Decorating Glass & Ceramics

HOW TO EMBELLISH GLASS,
CERAMIC, TERRACOTTA AND TILE
SURFACES WITH PAINT AND MOSAIC

Mary Fellows

LORENZ BOOKS

First published in 2001 by Lorenz Books

© Anness Publishing Limited 2001

Lorenz Books
is an imprint of
Anness Publishing Limited
Hermes House
88–89 Blackfriars Road
London SE1 8HA

This edition distributed in Canada by Raincoast Books,
9050 Shaughnessy Street, Vancouver, British Columbia V6P 6E5

Published in the USA by Lorenz Books, Anness Publishing Inc.,
27 West 20th Street, New York, NY 10011

A CIP catalogue record for this book is available
from the British Library

Publisher Joanna Lorenz
Managing Editor Helen Sudell
Project Editor Simona Hill
Text editors Heather Haynes and Kate Humby
Designer Nigel Partridge
Editorial Reader Diane Ashmore
Production Controller Ann Childers

10 9 8 7 6 5 4 3 2 1

Protective clothing should be worn when performing certain tasks described
in this book. Wear rubber (latex) gloves for grouting, using glass etching paste
and cleaning with hydrochloric acid; wear leather gloves when breaking
mosaic tesserae with a hammer; wear goggles when breaking tesserae with a
hammer, using tile nippers and cleaning with hydrochloric acid; wear a face
mask when sanding, cleaning with hydrochloric acid, cleaning lead with a wire
(steel) brush and working with the following: powdered grout, cement, sprays
(such as adhesive or varnish) and lead came.

Contents

Introduction

If you long to unleash your hidden creative talents but don't know where to begin then this book will provide plenty of ideas and inspiration to start you

off. Bursting with over 90 imaginative and clear step-by-step projects, there is something to suit all tastes and levels of ability.

Don't worry about your level of experience or artistic ability. Just look for the symbol at the start of each project. One brush indicates a project is relatively straightforward and can be easily tackled by a novice. Five brushes denote the most complex assignments, for which an advanced level of skill and knowledge is required. Whatever stage you are at, you will discover plenty of exciting projects to help stimulate your creativity, from simple hand-painted Mexican tiles to the more involved crazy paving chair. Whether you choose to begin with boldly painted ceramics or intricately pieced-together mosaics, each section will guide you through the basics, listing the tools

and materials you will require and explaining techniques specific to each craft.

Don't be deceived though – you really don't need any specialist artistic training to achieve the elaborate decorative effects shown.

Many projects utilize geometric shapes and freehand dots and swirls. You'll learn how to make printing blocks, use templates and stencils, cut mosaic tiles, create frosted and etched glass, and produce your own stained glass.

In no time at all, your home will be awash with the vibrant colours of boldly painted ceramics, mosaic mirrors, light-catching window hangings and festive glassware and crockery, and you'll be producing personalized gifts for friends and family.

Decorating
Ceramics

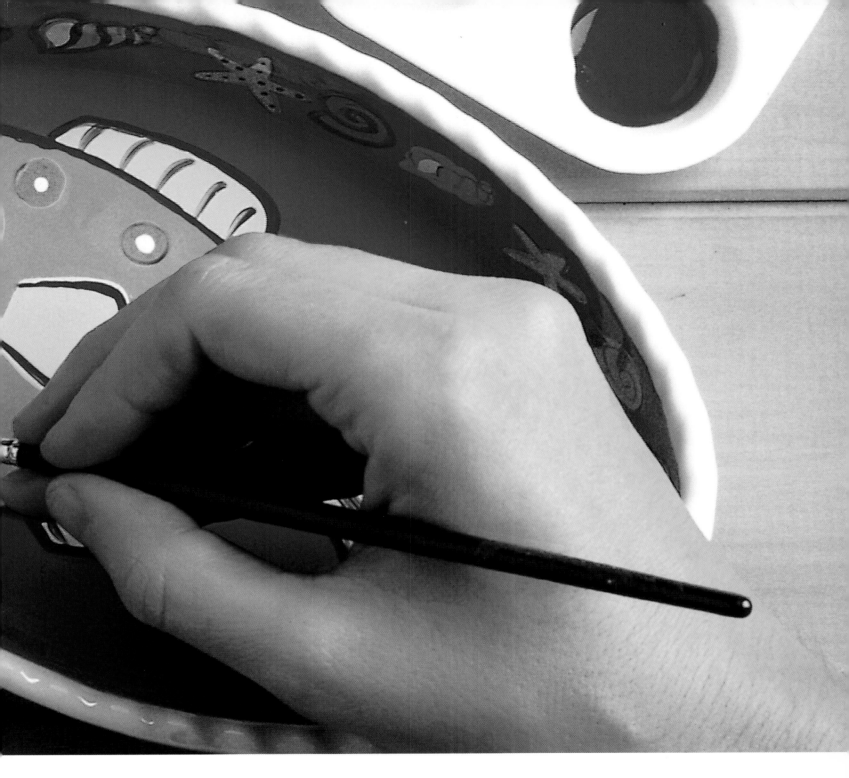

You do not need to be an expert artist or have trained drawing skills to paint beautiful designs on ceramics. All you need is the enthusiasm to have a go, and a design or a colour palette that will inspire you to follow through your idea. So even if you think you can't draw, there are templates to trace that take the hard work out of designing and will make colouring your design as easy as painting by numbers.

Cheerful China

Painting on ceramics is easy and great fun. It does not require any specialist artistic training and the motifs can be as simple as you like. Very little freehand painting is called for, as the designs are often repeating motifs which can be stencilled on the china, even on awkwardly-shaped items. Many of the projects in this chapter make use of templates which can be found at the back of the book. You can enlarge these to any size you like and use them to make stencils through which to paint your design.

There are also some patterns that are easy to paint freehand such as swirls, or dots, stripes and squares. Often, all a plain vase requires to brighten it up is a monochrome stripey border or a checked repeat pattern in bold primary colours. Some jugs, bowls and plates have a self-coloured low-relief pattern around the rim, which can offer a ready-made design for you to colour in.

If you are more adventurous and wish to try free-hand painting on plates and jugs (pitchers), keep your design simple. Naïve, simple motifs, such as

sunflowers, stars, fish and shells, make excellent decorative motifs and have a certain folk-art charm. Try to limit the number of colours you use, and keep colours bold and bright. Too much subtle shading does not work on ceramics – bold splashes of paint in two or three colours are more effective. Do not worry too much about neatness – the odd painting over a line or smudging of paint only adds to the hand-painted charm.

Many paints on the market designed for amateur painting on ceramics have to be baked to set, which can be done in a domestic oven. However, if the object is likely to come into contact with food or drink, the paint must first be fired in a pottery kiln or it will not be foodsafe.

In this chapter, you will find lots of ideas for painting plates, cups, saucers, vases, mugs and jugs. Have a go at some of the easier projects to get you started, then why not experiment with the template ideas, making up your own designs from different template combinations?

A variety of materials is needed for painting on ceramics, all of which are available from craft stores. Many items can be improvised, but some materials, such as paints, have to be specially purchased.

Materials

surfaces that may come in contact with foodstuffs or the mouth such as serving plates, bowls and cups.

Solvent-based ceramic paints

These come in a huge range of colours and lend themselves well to varied painting styles such as wash effects. White spirit (paint thinner) can be used to dilute the paint and to clean paintbrushes after use. Solvent-based paints take approximately 24 hours to dry. They can then be varnished to protect the finish.

Water-based ceramic paints

Sold under various trade names and specially made for painting glazed ceramics, these paints are available in a range of colours. They produce a strong, opaque, flat colour and can be diluted with water. Wash paintbrushes in warm water immediately after painting. Water-based paints dry in around 3 hours; do not attempt to bake them until they are completely dry or the colour may bubble. Baking the painted item will make the colour durable enough for a dishwasher. Put the item in a cold oven and do not remove it after baking until it has completely cooled. Always follow the paint manufacturer's instructions for the temperature and baking time, and do a test first as over-firing can turn the colour slightly brown.

Enamel paints

These paints are not made exclusively for china and ceramics. They are available in a range of colours and dry to a hard and durable finish. They contain lead and should only ever be used for decorative purposes and not on items that will contain food.

Masking fluid

Watercolour art masking fluid is used to mask off areas of the design while colour is applied to the surrounding area. Apply to a clean, dry surface. Always allow the masking fluid to dry before filling in the design with paint.

Polyurethane varnish and glazes

Apply varnish evenly, using a large, flat brush and stroking in one direction over the ceramic. The more coats you apply, the more durable and washable the surface, but keep each of the coats thin, allowing a minimum of 4 hours' drying time between coats. Polyurethane varnish is unsuitable for

No expensive specialist equipment is required for painting ceramics. In fact, you probably already have much of the equipment needed among your normal household supplies.

Equipment

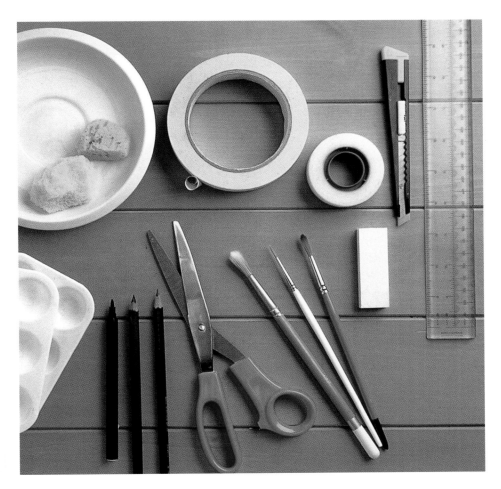

Paintbrushes
Use a fine brush for details, and a broad soft brush for covering larger areas.

Paint palette
Use to mix and hold paints.

Pencils and pens
A hard pencil is good for transferring designs; a soft for direct marking.

Printing blocks
Use for printing repeated patterns.

Ruler or straightedge
Plastic rules measure adequately. For cutting, metal ones are better.

Scissors
Use to cut paper patterns.

Self-healing cutting mat
This protects the work surface when cutting paper with a craft knife.

Stencil cardboard
This is manila card (cardboard) water-proofed with linseed oil.

Tracing paper
Use with carbon paper to transfer designs on to the object to be painted.

White spirit (paint thinner)
Use to clean brushes, to remove paint mistakes and to thin paint.

Carbon paper
Use to transfer designs on to ceramic. Place it carbon side down, on the object. Stick the image drawn on tracing paper on top. Draw over the image to transfer it to the ceramic.

Clear adhesive tape
Use for sticking designs to ceramic.

Craft knife
Use with a metal ruler and cutting mat for cutting papers and cardboard.

Masking film (frisket paper)
This self-adhesive transparent paper has a waxed paper backing, which peels away. Use it to mask out areas you want to keep blank.

Masking tape
Use to hold stencils in place and to mask off areas of ceramic.

Natural and synthetic sponges
Use to create paint effects for anything from an even to a textured finish.

The projects in this chapter do not require any specialist skills but it is worth practising a few painting techniques before you start. The tips suggested below will prove useful as you work through the ideas.

Techniques

Cleaning china

Before painting any white china, always clean it thoroughly to remove any invisible traces of dirt or grease. Effective cleaning agents are cleaning fluid, turpentine, methylated spirit (methyl alcohol), lighter fuel or white spirit (paint thinner). Keep these materials away from naked flames.

Safe drinking vessels

To ensure that there is no possibility of any paint being swallowed when drinking from a mug or glass, adapt designs so that any colour you paint is at least 3cm/1¼in below the rim of drinking vessels. Otherwise the piece should be fired in a kiln.

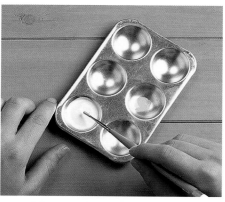

Working with paints

Paints suitable for applying to china are available in water or oil-based types. When mixing up a shade of your own, remember that the two types of paint cannot be intermixed. Always thoroughly clean brushes as directed by the paint manufacturer.

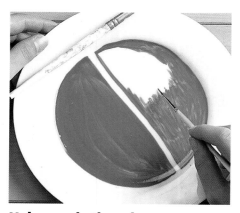

Using paintbrushes

Always use an appropriately sized paintbrush for the task in hand. Larger areas should always be painted with a large brush using bold strokes, while small, fine brushes are best for all detailed work.

Watery effects

You can achieve a watery effect in oil-based colours by diluting paints with white spirit (paint thinner). Water-based paints can be diluted by adding water.

Creating white lines

If you want to leave thin lines of china showing through areas of colour, paint them in first with masking fluid. This can be gently peeled off when the paint is dry to reveal the white china beneath. Use an instrument with a sharp point such as a craft knife or compass to lift off the dried masking fluid.

Using masking fluid

Add a drop of water-based paint to masking fluid before use when you are working on plain white china. This will help you to see where the masking fluid has been applied, enabling you to wipe it off easily when you are ready to do so.

Preparing a sponge

Use a craft knife to cut cubes of sponge for sponging paint. Hold the sponge taut as you slice down into it to make cutting easier and the lines straight. Keep several sponge cubes to hand when sponging as you may need to change them frequently.

Testing a sponge

Before sponging on to your china after loading the sponge with paint, test the print on a scrap piece of paper. The first print or two will be too saturated with paint to achieve a pleasing effect.

Sponging variations

A stencilled design can be made more interesting by varying the density of the sponging within the image or by adding more than one colour. Allow the first coat of paint to dry partially before the application of the second.

Printing blocks

Test the print on scrap paper before you print on the china. When using printing blocks, roll the block lightly on to the surface to ensure you get a good, even print.

Straight lines

Masking tape is useful for painting straight edges, stripes and even checks and squares. Just stick it down to mark out areas you do not want painted and apply the paint. Remove the tape before the paint is completely dry; straight lines of paint will be left.

Removing masking tape or film

When using masking tape or film (frisket paper), it is better to remove it before the paint is completely dry as this will give a cleaner edge to the pattern beneath.

Tracing

Use tracing paper and a soft pencil to transfer designs directly on to china. First trace the template or the design you wish to use, then fix the tracing paper to the china with pieces of masking tape. Rub over the traced design with a soft pencil to transfer.

Removing guide markings

Pencil or pen guide marks on the china are easy to wipe off once the paint is completely dry or has been baked. Use a damp paper towel or cloth and take care not to rub the paint too hard.

Testing new techniques

Always test out a technique that you have not tried before. Apply the new technique to a spare piece of china, which can be cleaned up easily, rather than to a piece you are already in the process of decorating.

Removing unwanted paint

Use a pencil eraser or cotton buds (swabs) to tidy up a design or to wipe off small areas of unwanted paint. For larger areas use a damp paper towel or cloth. Allow the cleaned area to dry before repainting.

Preparing a stencil

A stencil is a thin sheet with a decorative pattern cut out, through which paint is applied. This can be used to repeat the pattern on a chosen surface. Try designing and making your own.

1 To transfer a template on to a piece of stencil cardboard, place a piece of tracing paper over the design, and draw over it with a hard pencil.

2 Turn over the tracing paper, and on the back of the design rub over the lines you have drawn with a pencil.

3 Turn the tracing paper back to the right side and place on top of a sheet of stencil cardboard. Draw over the original lines with a hard pencil.

4 To cut out the stencil, place the stencil on to a cutting mat or piece of thick cardboard and tape in place. Use a craft knife for cutting.

5 To transfer a detailed design using carbon paper, place the stencil over a piece of carbon paper, carbon side down. Attach the carbon paper to the china piece with masking tape. Use a soft pencil to trace the shape lightly on to the china.

Stencilling offers a quick and easy method of decorating china. The simple shapes of these limes look terrific adorning a fruit bowl. Choose just two or three bold colours for maximum effect.

Citrus Fruit Bowl

You will need

soft pencil
tracing paper
masking tape
stencil cardboard
self-healing cutting mat
craft knife
plain fruit bowl
cleaning fluid
cloth
yellow chinagraph pencil
water-based ceramic paints: citrus
green, mid-green, dark green
and yellow
paint palette
artist's paintbrushes
acrylic varnish (optional)

1 Draw a freehand lime shape on to tracing paper. Using masking tape to hold the tracing paper securely in place, transfer the lime outline to a piece of stencil cardboard. Working on a self-healing cutting mat, carefully cut all around the shape of the lime using a craft knife with a sharp blade.

2 Clean a plain fruit bowl. Attach the stencil to the bowl using masking tape. Draw inside the stencil outline on to the bowl using a yellow chinagraph pencil. Repeat to draw several limes all over the bowl.

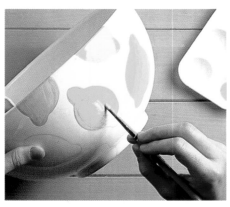

3 Fill in all the lime shapes with citrus green paint using an artist's paintbrush. Allow the paint to dry completely. Add highlights to each of the fruits using the mid-green paint and allow the paint to dry thoroughly as before.

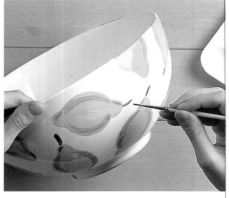

4 Paint a stalk at the end of each lime shape in the dark green paint. Allow to dry. Paint the background all over the outside of the bowl yellow, leaving a thin white outline around each of the lime shapes to help them stand out.

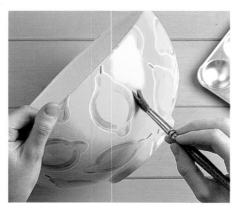

5 To complete the bowl, either use a clean brush to apply a coat of acrylic varnish over the painted section, or bake the bowl in the oven, following the paint manufacturer's instructions.

Add colour to a plain white dinner service by embellishing it with ceramic paints. Vary the motifs, or use just one per plate, so that each place setting is different.

Seashore-style China

You will need
tracing paper
soft pencil
scissors
china plates and soup bowls
cloth
cleaning fluid
ruler
carbon paper
masking tape
blue solvent-based ceramic paint
fine artist's paintbrush
cloth

1 Copy the templates from the back of the book on to tracing paper. Cut out the shapes with scissors. Clean the plate thoroughly with a cloth and cleaning fluid.

2 To decorate a plate, find and mark the middle with a ruler and pencil. Divide the plate into eight equal parts and lightly mark up the eight sections in pencil.

3 If you make plenty of copies of each design, you can use your templates to experiment with various design options.

4 Cut a piece of carbon paper into small pieces to fit your templates.

5 Place the carbon paper under the template designs on the plate and stick them down firmly with masking tape to secure.

6 Trace around the template outlines with a sharp pencil, then remove the masking tape, templates and carbon paper to reveal the design.

7 Paint in the shapes carefully using blue solvent-based ceramic paint. Leave to dry thoroughly.

8 Mark, trace and paint the design in the centre of the soup bowl. Add small dots on the handles of the bowl. Leave to dry. Remove the pencil lines.

Ceramics with low-relief decorative motifs are ideal for painting. Like children's colouring books, the shapes are all set out ready to colour in and, as there are no clearly defined outlines, mistakes will go unnoticed.

Low-relief Ceramic

You will need

clean, white glazed pitcher with a low-relief fruit motif
medium and fine artist's paintbrushes
solvent-based ceramic paints: acid yellow, golden yellow, light green, medium green and dark green
polyurethane varnish or glaze

1 Paint some of the lemons on the pitcher acid yellow. Vary them so that one group has two acid yellow lemons, the next group one, and so on. Leave a narrow white line around each lemon, and leave the seed cases and the small circles at the base of the fruit white. Allow to dry.

2 Work your way around the relief pattern at the top of the pitcher, painting the remaining fruit a rich golden yellow. Using two yellows for the fruit creates a sense of depth and variety. Once again, leave a narrow white line around each fruit, and leave the paint to dry.

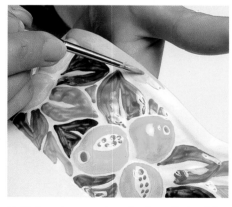

3 Starting with light green, paint roughly a third of the leaves, evenly spaced apart if possible, but don't worry about being too exact. Leave the central midrib of each leaf and a narrow line around each leaf white. Allow to dry. Paint the small circles.

4 Paint a third of the leaves medium green, spacing them evenly. Paint a narrow green line around the base of the pitcher and leave to dry. Paint the remaining leaves dark green and leave to dry.

5 Paint the rim (or the handle) of the pitcher in acid yellow, leaving a narrow white line at the lower edge. Once the paint is dry, varnish the pitcher with polyurethane varnish or the glaze provided specially by the ceramic paint manufacturer for this purpose.

Imagine the effect produced by a whole set of this delightful sponge-ware design, set out on your kitchen shelves. Painting your own mugs in this lovely decorative style is an easy way of transforming plain china.

Stamped Spongeware

You will need
ballpoint pen
cellulose kitchen sponge
scissors
all-purpose glue
corrugated cardboard
ceramic paints: dark blue and
dark green
paint palette
kitchen paper
clean, white china mugs
masking tape
craft knife
fine black felt-tipped pen
stencil brush or small
cosmetic sponge

1 Draw a crab on the sponge. Cut out and glue to the corrugated cardboard. Trim as close as possible. Press the sponge into the blue paint and blot any excess on kitchen paper. Stamp the crab evenly on to the mugs.

2 Allow the paint to dry. Stick the masking tape around the bottom edge of the mug. Draw the border freehand on the tape with black felt-tipped pen. Carefully cut away the bottom edge of the masking tape using a craft knife.

3 Use the cosmetic sponge to decorate the border. Use both the blue and green paints, to add depth. Sponge the handles and stamp more mugs with related motifs. Peel off the masking tape. Set the paints.

A set of delicately frosted plates would look terrific for winter dinner settings and this snowflake design is child's play to achieve. Make up as many differently designed snowflakes as you like.

Sponged Snowflake Plate

You will need

plain china plate

cleaning fluid

cloth

pencil

cup

masking film (frisket paper)

scissors

craft knife

self-healing cutting mat

sponge

paint dish

water-based ceramic paints: ice blue, dark blue and gold

1 Clean the plate. Draw round an upturned cup on to the backing paper of masking film (frisket paper) to make eight circles. Cut out the circles with scissors. Fold each circle in half. Crease each semi-circle twice to make three equal sections. Fold these sections over each other to make a triangle with a curved edge.

2 Draw a partial snowflake design on to one triangle and shade the areas that will be cut away. Ensure that parts of the folded edges remain intact. Cut out the design using a craft knife and self-healing cutting mat. Repeat to make seven more snowflake shapes. Unfold them, peel away the backing paper and position them on the plate.

3 Load a sponge cube with ice blue paint and dab it all over the plate. When dry, sponge darker blue around the outer and inner rims. Allow to dry, then dab a sponge loaded with gold paint around the edge of the plate, the inner rim and dark areas to highlight them. Remove the film snowflakes and then set the paint following the manufacturer's instructions.

Jazz up herb containers to match your kitchen decor. Each of these jars bears a coloured panel which can be used to display the name of the herb contained within.

Kitchen Herb Jars

You will need
tracing paper
soft pencil
carbon paper
masking tape
6 plain china herb jars
cleaning fluid
cloth
blue chinagraph pencil
water-based enamel paints: blue, lime green, dark green and turquoise
paint palette
artist's paintbrush
dried-out felt-tipped pen

1 Draw one large and one small leaf design, each on a separate piece of tracing paper. Attach the tracing paper to carbon paper, carbon side down, with masking tape.

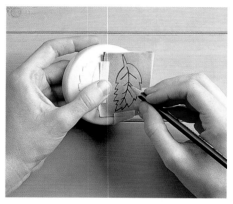

2 Clean the jars. Attach the tracing of the larger leaf on to the lid of a jar, to one side, and trace the outline with a pencil to transfer the design. Replace the tracing in another position on the lid and repeat.

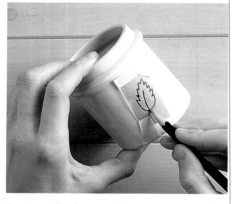

3 Attach the smaller tracing to the side of a jar and trace the leaf outline on to the jar. Repeat the process to transfer the outline several times in different places around the jar, leaving a large space in the centre of one side for the "lozenge".

4 Using a blue chinagraph pencil, draw a freehand oval shape in the large space you have left. Fill in the oval with blue paint.

5 Before the paint dries, draw a design, pattern or a word on the oval shape, using an old dried-out felt-tipped pen. The felt tip will remove the blue paint to reveal the white china beneath.

6 Paint the herb leaves lime green. Allow the paint to dry completely. Add detail to the leaves in a darker green paint. Allow to dry.

7 Fill in the background in turquoise, leaving a thin white outline around each image. Paint the background of the lid in the same way. Leave the paint to dry. Paint the remaining jars in complementary colours.

The colour scheme of this decorative wall plate is inspired by the rich colours of medieval tapestries. Solvent-based paints are used as they are available in metallic colours which can be diluted.

Heraldic Wall Plate

You will need
large, shallow, white-glazed plate
self-sticking dots
scissors
medium and fine artist's paintbrushes
solvent-based ceramic paint: yellow,
red, gold, black and green
turpentine or clear rubbing alcohol
craft knife
hard pencil
tracing paper
pair of compasses (compass)
carbon paper
masking tape
polyurethane varnish or glaze

1 Stick small, sticky-backed dots at random over the middle of the plate. Cut some more of the dots in half, and stick them around the natural edge of the centre, where it meets the rim section of the plate. Press them down firmly.

2 Paint a small area of the centre with a thick coat of yellow solvent-based ceramic paint. Dip the paintbrush in turpentine or rubbing alcohol and spread the paint for a colourwashed effect. Work outwards to the edge of the centre section. Leave to dry.

3 Carefully remove the sticky-backed dots using the edge of a craft knife. If any of the yellow paint has bled under the dots, use a fine paintbrush dipped in solvent to remove it, so that you are left with a clean outline around all the white circles.

4 Using the same colourwashing technique, paint the rim of the plate red. Paint up to the yellow; do not worry if you go slightly over it. Leave the red paint to dry. Draw around the rim of the plate on to tracing paper. Measure and draw the central circle of the plate on to the tracing paper with a pair of compasses.

5 Cut out the outer ring of tracing paper and fold into eighths. The folds mark the top of each fleur-de-lis. Cut a carbon paper ring the same size. Place it face down on the rim and fix with masking tape. Open out the tracing paper and tape on top. Mark the points on the plate. Remove the carbon and tracing paper.

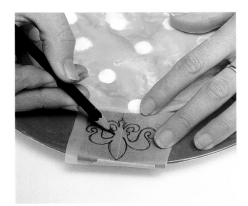

6 Using the template provided, draw a fleur-de-lis, slightly smaller than the rim depth, on to tracing paper. Cut a square of carbon paper the same size. Align the motif with a mark. Securing with masking tape, slip the carbon paper underneath. Transfer to the plate. Repeat around the rim.

7 Using gold paint, paint the fleur-de-lis motifs, the centres of the white dots, and dots between the fleur-de-lis. The gold ceramic paint will be quite translucent, and you may have to paint two coats, especially over the red, to achieve a rich tone. Allow the paint to dry between coats.

8 Using a fine paintbrush and black paint, carefully work around the fleur-de-lis motifs and the white dots to create a crisp outline. Leave the paint to dry.

9 Using a medium paintbrush, paint a green line all around the edge of the yellow circle. Try to keep the line as even as possible. You may find it easier with a fine paintbrush, going round two or three times. Cover the paint with varnish or glaze.

Brighten up a plain china lampbase with a series of quirky patterns in bright turquoise, pink, lime and lilac. You will need to dismantle the base before painting it.

Patterned Lampbase

You will need

ceramic lampbase

cleaning fluid

cloth

soft pencil

tracing paper

plain paper

scissors

carbon paper

clear adhesive tape

solvent-based ceramic paints: lilac, turquoise, pink, lime and black

medium and fine artist's paintbrushes

lampshade

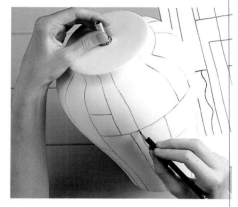

1 Clean the lampbase and remove all the electrics. Trace the background template from the back of the book on to tracing paper and transfer to a piece of paper. Using the paper as a guide, transfer the background design on to the lampbase with a soft pencil.

2 Trace the pattern templates at the back of the book on to tracing paper and transfer on to a sheet of plain paper. Cut out the designs, and attach them to carbon paper using clear adhesive tape.

3 Paint the background of the lampbase using a medium paintbrush. First paint in the lilac sections, then add the turquoise, pink and lime. Leave the paint to dry.

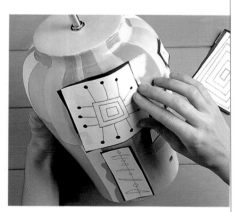

4 Arrange the designs around the painted lampbase, then fix them in place with clear adhesive tape. Use a soft pencil to transfer the design through the carbon paper on to the lampbase. Press lightly on the plain paper to leave a clear print.

5 Using the black ceramic paint and a fine paintbrush, work carefully over the outlines made by the carbon paper. When the paint is completely dry, refit the electrics to the lampbase and attach a lampshade in a complementary colour.

Coffee cups handpainted with broad brush strokes and lots of little raised dots of paint are simpler to create than you would think...with the help of a little self-adhesive vinyl.

Leaf Motif Cup and Saucer

You will need

white ceramic cup and saucer

cleaning fluid

cloth

cotton buds (swabs)

pencil

paper

scissors

self-adhesive vinyl

green water-based ceramic paint

medium artist's paintbrush

hair dryer (optional)

craft knife

pewter acrylic paint with nozzle-tipped tube

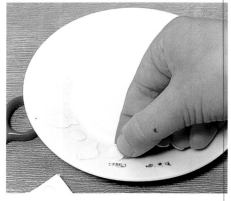

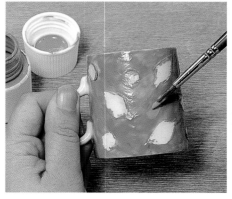

1 Clean any grease from the china to be painted using cleaning fluid and a cloth or cotton bud (swab). Draw leaves and circles freehand on to paper. Cut them out and draw around them on the backing of the self-adhesive vinyl. Cut out. Peel away the backing paper and stick the pieces on the china.

2 Paint around the leaf and circle shapes with green water-based ceramic paint, applying several coats of paint in order to achieve a solid colour. Leave the centre circle of the saucer white. Leave each coat to air-dry before applying the next, or use a hair dryer for speed.

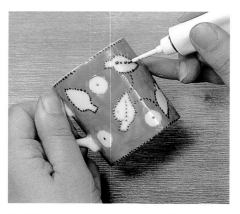

3 To ensure that the design has a tidy edge, cut around each sticky shape carefully with a craft knife, then peel off the sticky-backed plastic.

4 Clean up any smudges with a cotton bud dipped in acetone or water. Paint fine green lines out from the centre of each circle.

5 Using pewter paint and the nozzle-tipped paint tube, mark the outlines and details of the leaves with rows of small dots. Leave for 36 hours, then bake, following the manufacturer's instructions. The paint will withstand everyday use, but not the dishwasher.

Sunflowers seem to be perennially popular as decorating motifs. They certainly make a wonderfully cheerful design. Be adventurous and try your hand at this freehand decoration.

Sunflower Vase

You will need
plain white ceramic vase
cleaning fluid
cloth
tracing paper
soft pencil
masking tape
chinagraph pencils: yellow and blue
water-based enamel paints: yellow,
pale green, light brown, dark green,
very pale brown and sky blue
paint palette
medium and fine artist's paintbrushes

1 Clean the vase thoroughly. Draw a freehand sunflower on to the tracing paper and enlarge it if necessary. Fix the tracing to the vase using masking tape, and rub with a soft pencil to transfer the image.

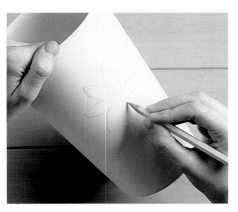

2 Reposition the tracing paper to transfer the sunflower design all around the vase. Highlight the outline of each design with a yellow chinagraph pencil.

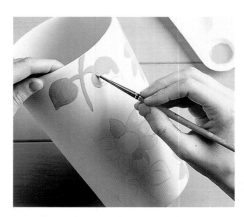

3 Fill in the petals with yellow paint and the stalks and leaves with pale green. Allow to dry. Paint the flower-head centres light brown. Include a circle of short lines around the edge of each flower centre. Allow to dry.

4 Add detail to the leaves using a darker shade of green. Add dabs of very pale brown to the centre of each flowerhead. Allow to dry. Fill in the background with sky blue paint, leaving a white edge showing around the flower. Allow to dry.

5 Finally, draw around the outline and central detail of each flower with a blue chinagraph pencil.

Imaginative seaside designs applied to a plain ceramic soap dish and toothbrush holder will transform the look of your bathroom, giving it an underwater theme.

Seashore Bathroom Set

You will need

plain china soap dish and
toothbrush holder or mug

cleaning fluid

cloth

tracing paper

soft and hard pencils

plain paper

adhesive spray

carbon paper

scissors or craft knife

masking tape

medium and fine artist's paintbrushes

water-based ceramic paints: mid-blue,
ivory, turquoise, lemon, pink,
white and dark blue

paint palette

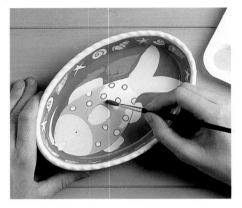

1 Clean the china well. Trace the templates at the back of the book, enlarging if necessary. Transfer the designs on to plain paper. Spray the back of the paper with adhesive and stick to the back of a sheet of carbon paper. Cut out the designs, leaving a margin all round. Tape on to the china; transfer the lines with a hard pencil. Remove the carbon.

2 Using a medium paintbrush, paint a border around the soap dish, and then paint the background in mid-blue. When it is dry, paint the fish and shells, using the ivory, turquoise, lemon and pink paints. Paint the toothbrush holder in the same way.

3 When the paint is completely dry, add the final touches to the soap dish and toothbrush holder. Paint on white dots and fine squiggles to create the effect of water. Using a fine paintbrush and the dark blue paint, carefully sketch in any detailing on the fish and shells. Allow to dry.

This cheerful sun design would be particularly welcome on the breakfast table for milk, orange juice or a simple posy of flowers. The colours could be adapted to suit your other china.

Morning Sun Face

You will need

white ceramic jug (pitcher)

cleaning fluid

cloth

tracing paper

hard and soft pencils

scissors

masking tape

acrylic china paints: black, bright yellow, ochre, blue, red and white

paint palette

fine artist's paintbrushes

hair dryer (optional)

2 Go over the sun's outlines with black paint and allow to dry; a hair dryer can speed up the process. Paint the main face and inner rays in bright yellow and then paint the cheeks and other parts of the rays in ochre.

3 Paint the background blue, then add fine details to the sun's face. Highlight each eye with a white dot. Set, following the manufacturer's instructions. The paint will withstand everyday use, but not the dishwasher.

1 Clean the china to remove any grease. Trace the template at the back of the book, try it for size and enlarge it if necessary. Cut it out roughly then rub over the back with a soft pencil. Make several cuts around the edge of the circle, so that the template will lie flat, and tape it in place. Draw over the outlines with a hard pencil to transfer the design.

The application of a few gold blocks of colour, highlighted by sketched leaf outlines which are positioned like falling leaves, quickly turns a plain white coffee pot into an elegant piece of ceramic ware.

Autumn Leaf Coffee Pot

You will need

hard and soft pencils
stencil cardboard
craft knife
metal ruler
self-healing cutting mat
carbon paper
fine felt-tipped pen
plain ceramic coffee pot
cleaning fluid
cloth
masking tape
sponge
water-based ceramic paints:
gold and black
paint dish
fine artist's paintbrush

1 Use a pencil to draw an irregular four-sided shape, approximately 2cm/ ¾in square, on to a piece of stencil cardboard. Using a sharp craft knife, a metal ruler and self-healing cutting mat, cut the shape away, leaving the cardboard border intact.

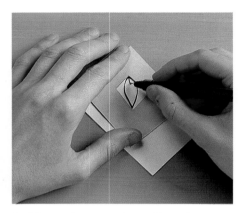

2 Place the stencil cardboard over a piece of carbon paper, carbon side down. Gently draw the outline of a leaf with a centre vein through the stencil hole on to the piece of carbon paper, using a fine felt-tipped pen.

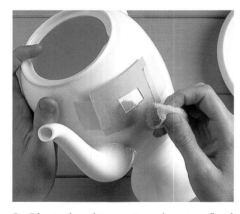

3 Clean the china using cleaning fluid and a cloth. Attach the stencil to the pot with masking tape. Load a small sponge cube with gold paint. Lightly dab it over the stencil, without going over the outside edge of the cardboard. Leave to dry. Remove the stencil.

4 Replace the stencil in a new position on the coffee pot, rotating it slightly. Avoid sticking the masking tape over the previously painted shape. Dab the stencil with gold paint as before. Repeat the process to create a random pattern over the entire coffee pot, including the spout and lid.

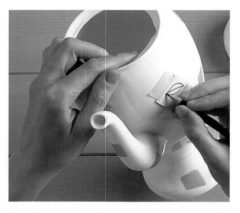

5 Using masking tape, carefully attach the carbon paper with the leaf drawing over a stencilled gold shape so that the leaf outline overlaps the edge of colour. With a sharp soft pencil, lightly transfer the leaf shape on to the coffee pot.

6 Remove the carbon paper and trace the shape over the remaining blocks of gold colour. Position the leaves at slightly different angles each time.

7 Darken the leaf outlines with black paint, using a fine paintbrush. Leave to dry. Fill in the leaf veins with black paint. Leave to dry.

8 Finish off the design by painting the knob of the coffee pot lid with gold paint. Allow to dry.

Stylized holly leaves and berries decorate the rim of this festive oval platter, while the gold outlines and gold-spattered centre add seasonal glamour. Display this painted plate heaped high with mince pies.

Holly Christmas Platter

You will need
white glazed oval plate
masking film (frisket paper)
scissors
craft knife
hard and soft pencils
watercolour paper or
flexible cardboard
fine felt-tipped pen (optional)
medium and fine artist's paintbrushes
solvent-based ceramic paints: rich dark
green, bright red, maroon, gold
white spirit (paint thinner)
toothbrush
paint palette
polyurethane varnish

1 Cut out a rectangle of masking film (frisket paper), roughly the size of the plate. Take the backing off and stick on to the plate, pressing it outwards from the centre. Using a craft knife, cut around the inner oval edge of the rim to mask out the plate centre. Remove the excess.

2 Using the template provided, draw two or three holly leaves with an elongated oval for the midrib on to watercolour paper or flexible cardboard. Give the leaves different curving shapes to add interest. Cut out the leaves and centres using a craft knife or small sharp scissors.

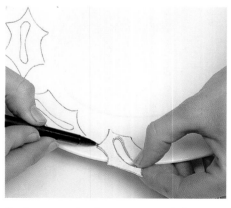

3 Arrange the leaves around the rim, leaving room for stems and a line at the top and bottom of the rim. Mark with a pencil where the first leaf starts. Fill in any space with extra berries. Draw around the leaves using a fine felt-tipped pen or pencil.

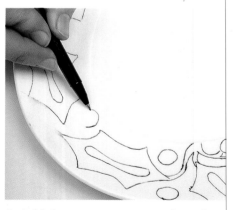

4 Add the stems, some straight, others curved, some single, others joining to form sprigs. To fill the gaps, draw berries singly or in pairs.

5 Using a medium paintbrush, paint the holly leaves and stems green, leaving the midrib white. Allow to dry, then add touches of green to highlight. Allow to dry, then paint the berries red and leave to dry.

6 Paint the maroon background. Use a fine paintbrush to go round the leaves, stems and berries first, leaving a narrow white outline, as shown. Infill the awkward background spaces with a fine paintbrush, then switch to a medium paintbrush for the rest. Allow to dry.

7 Using a medium paintbrush, paint a gold outline around the leaves and berries, and along one side of the stems. Try to leave as much white outline as possible exposed. Leave to dry. Using the edge of a craft knife, lift the masking paper off the middle of the plate.

8 To spatter the platter gold, mix two parts paint to one part white spirit (paint thinner). Pour a little paint into a saucer, and then spatter the platter with gold by rubbing your thumb over a toothbrush dipped in paint. Leave to dry. Paint a narrow red band around the rim. When dry, coat with varnish.

Imagine the delight this painted tea set featuring playful rabbits will bring to a child you know. This fun design is easy to accomplish using the templates provided; they can be enlarged as necessary.

Fun Bunnies Tea Set

You will need

plain china mug, plate and bowl

cleaning fluid

cloth

tracing paper

soft pencil

plain paper

adhesive spray

carbon paper

scissors

clear adhesive tape

felt-tipped pen

cotton bud (swab)

water-based enamel paints: yellow, turquoise, red, green and blue

paint palette

medium and fine artist's paintbrushes

1 Thoroughly clean the china mug, plate and bowl with cleaning fluid and a cloth. Trace the templates for the rabbits and flower at the back of the book and transfer them to a piece of plain paper. Spray the back of the paper with glue and place it on top of a sheet of carbon paper, carbon side down. Cut out around the drawings, leaving a narrow margin.

2 Arrange the cut-out drawings around the china mug, plate and bowl, securing them in place with clear adhesive tape. Go over the designs with a felt-tipped pen to transfer the designs to the china pieces. Remove the cut-outs and clean any smudges carefully with a cotton bud (swab).

3 Paint the background areas of the centre of the bowl in yellow.

4 Paint the remaining background areas, around the rim of the bowl, in turquoise. Leave to dry.

5 Begin to paint in the details. Here the flowers are painted red, turquoise and green.

◀ **6** Using a fine paintbrush, paint over the outlines of the large rabbits and flowers with blue paint. Paint over the outlines of the smaller rabbits on the rim of the plate with blue paint.

▶ **7** Paint the mug handle turquoise. Allow to dry. The pieces should be fired in a kiln to make them foodsafe.

Kitchen storage jars are always useful, and when adorned with bold designs such as these colourful vegetables they add quirky visual detail to your kitchen.

Vegetable Storage Jars

You will need
tracing paper
soft pencil
plain paper
adhesive spray
carbon paper
scissors
plain china storage jars
cleaning fluid
cloth
clear adhesive tape
felt-tipped pen
medium and fine artist's paintbrushes
water-based enamel paints: turquoise, coral, ivory, blue and yellow
paint palette

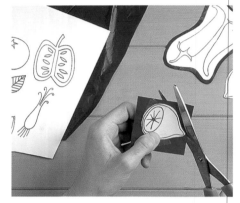

1 Trace the templates at the back of the book and enlarge if necessary. Transfer the designs on to a piece of plain paper. Spray the back of the paper with glue and stick it on to a sheet of carbon paper, carbon side down. Cut out the designs leaving a margin all round.

2 Clean the china storage jars, using cleaning fluid and a cloth. Tape some of the designs on to one of the jars. Go over the outlines lightly with a felt-tipped pen to transfer the designs to the jar. Remove the carbon paper designs and repeat the process for the other jars.

3 Using a medium paintbrush, paint in the turquoise background colour between the vegetable designs on the sides of the storage jars and their lids. Allow the paint to dry completely before proceeding to the next stage – this may take several days.

4 Mix up some red paint from the coral and ivory and paint the chillies. Mix the blue and yellow paint and paint the green of the vegetable leaves. Allow to dry.

5 Using a fine paintbrush and the blue paint, sketch in the detailing for the vegetables.

6 Paint the jar rims with the yellow paint and add some small ivory dots in the turquoise background area for decoration. Allow the paint to dry completely before using the jars.

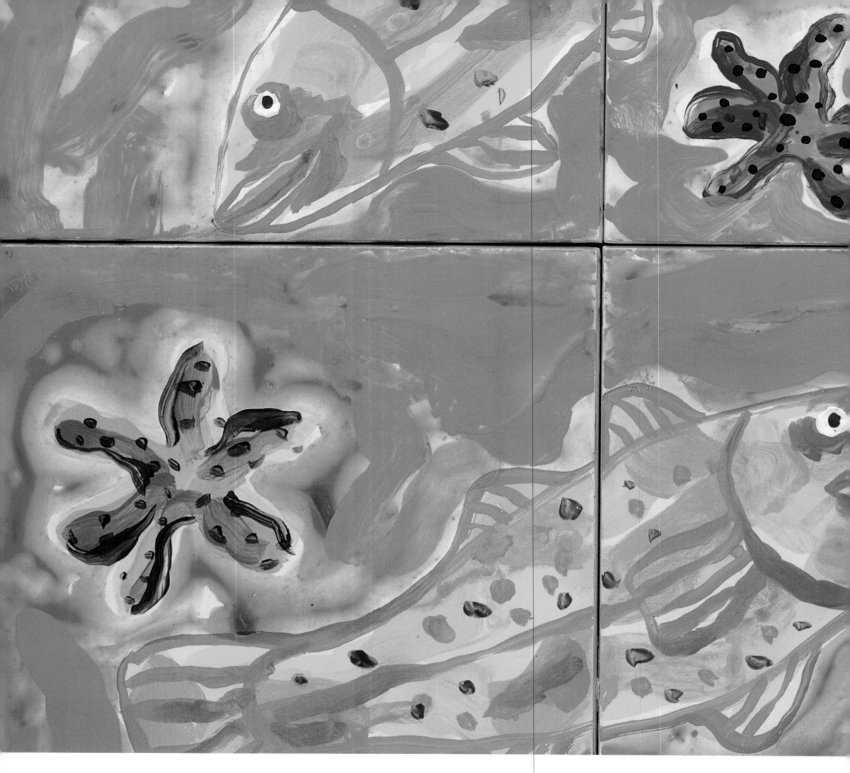

Decorating Tiles

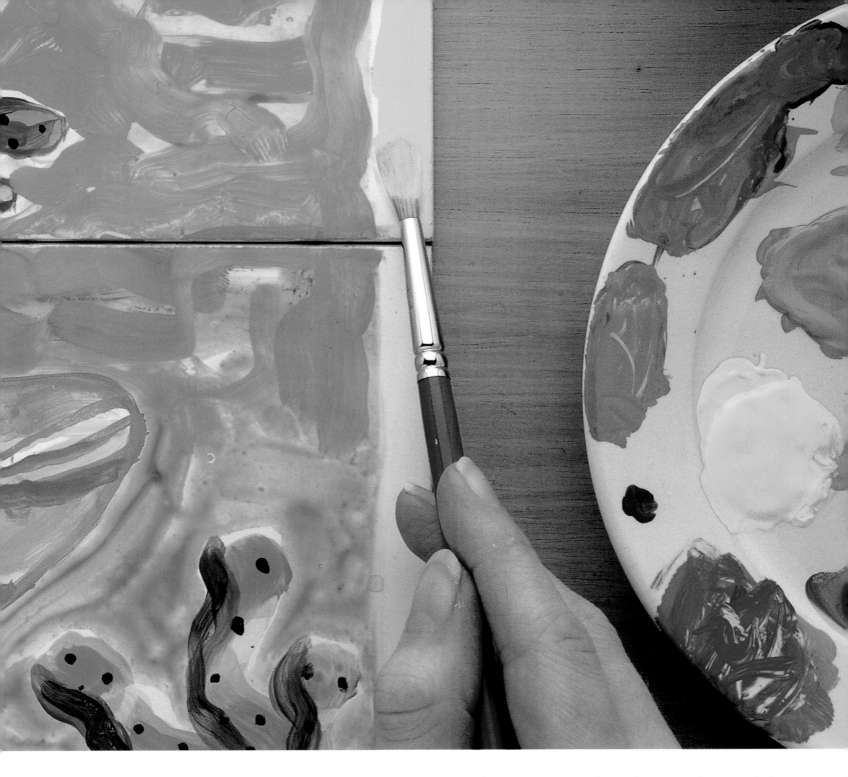

Plain white glazed tiles offer perfect blank canvases for decorating with paint, and their flat surface makes it so easy to do. Use single tiles for pot or pan stands, or plan a small-scale panel design over four or six tiles to add decorative details to plain walls, floors and splashbacks. Like ceramics, tiles can be decorated in a myriad ways, using different techniques and finishes depending upon their intended use.

Tiles with Style

As with painting on ceramics, painting on tiles is quick and fun to do, and because of the tile's flat surface, it is so much easier. No great artistic skill is called for and if you make a mistake you can simply wash it off and start again. You can unleash your creative side by painting anything from bright and colourful patterns with bold brushstrokes to finely detailed floral patterns, or make an elaborate silver decoupage masterpiece. If you prefer paint effects to patterns or motifs, tiles make wonderful surfaces for printing, sponging, spattering and stencilling.

Many of the projects in this chapter have templates for you to follow so you can reproduce the design featured. In this way you can create wonderful cherubs, Byzantine birds, Art Nouveau designs and even a William Morris-

style tile. Yet there are also ideas for less ambitious schemes, such as tiles depicting colourful cartoon characters or alphabet letters for a child's room, or pretty rosebud tiles for a feminine bathroom or bedroom.

Some of the projects feature individual tiles, the design of which can be repeated to make several similar tiles to use in a decorative border, or set at random in a wall or splashback of plain-coloured tiles. Other projects feature a group of tiles that are

made up into a panel, with the design travelling across six or eight tiles. These can be attached to a backing board and hung in place of a painting or wallhanging, rather than being used for practical purposes. Painted tiles can also make an excellent decorative border around a room, for example set just above a skirting (base) board, shelf or mantelpiece. They can also be used to decorate the top of a

cupboard, dressing table or coffee table. Provided the tiles are grouted correctly, they will provide a wipe-clean surface.

This chapter contains plenty of ideas for design and colour combinations to inspire you, or you can adapt the designs to suit your own colour schemes and, if you are feeling adventurous, you can dream up your own designs and motifs.

White, glazed tiles are inexpensive, making this craft truly accessible to everyone. Painted tiles can add instant cheer to a room and help to complement existing features and fittings.

Materials

Ceramic wall tiles

Glazed wall tiles are waterproof and hardwearing, though brittle. They are thinner than floor tiles, usually about 5mm/¼in thick, and come in a huge range of colours, designs, finishes and sizes. The tiles used the most in this chapter are plain white tiles as they allow plenty of scope for decoration.

Cold-set ceramic paints

Ceramic paints that are non-toxic, water-based and cold-set are the choice recommended for painting tiles. They are available in a wide range of colours and can be mixed or thinned with water. The paints set to a very durable finish after 48–72 hours drying time, but they are not as durable as unpainted glazed tiles. Care must be taken when grouting – keep the grout to the edges of the tile only. Do not clean the tiles vigorously but wipe them with a damp cloth. If more permanent decoration is required, heat-fixable paints that are set in a domestic oven are available. Make sure your tiles are sturdy enough to be heated in this way.

Masking tape

This removable paper tape is available in different widths. It is used to mask off areas to be painted, and also to hold stencils and tracings in place.

PVA (white) glue

Use this to attach decoupage images.

Ready-mixed and powdered grout and colourant

Powdered grout is more economical than ready-mixed grout. Mix with water to a creamy paste, following the manufacturer's instructions. Powdered grout comes in different colours, or can also be coloured with grout colourant. Wear a protective face mask, safety goggles and rubber (latex) gloves when handling or mixing powdered materials.

Stencil cardboard

This manila cardboard has been impregnated with oil and is available in several thicknesses. It is durable and water-resistant and it makes strong stencils with crisp edges that last well. The cardboard is easy to cut with a craft knife and cutting mat.

Tile adhesive

Use this to glue tiles to the wall.

You will not need to purchase many items of equipment for painting tiles, but try to ensure you buy good quality paintbrushes for the most professional finish.

Equipment

Self-healing cutting mat
Use this mat to protect your work surface when cutting anything with a craft knife.

Set square
Use to align guide battens and to check that each row of tiles is straight.

Spirit (carpenter's) level
This will ensure a straight line when you are fixing a guide batten.

Sponge
Use a damp sponge to remove excess tile adhesive and grout from tiles.

Tile spacers
These are small plastic crosses that are placed between tiles to create regular gaps for grouting. They are useful if you are using tiles without in-built spacer lugs. Some spacers are removed before grouting after the adhesive has dried. Others are much thinner and can simply be grouted over.

Tracing paper
Use to trace motifs from the back of the book and transfer to plain tiles.

You will also find the following items useful: face mask, hammer, hand-held tile cutter, leather gloves, paintbrushes, pencils, rubber (latex) gloves, tile-cutting machine, tile file.

Craft knife
This tool is very useful for making clean, precise cuts. Always cut away from your body and use a metal ruler to cut against.

Lint-free cloth
Use for polishing tiles after grouting.

Metal ruler
This is very useful for marking out guidelines for cutting stencils or for other decoration.

Notched spreader
Use to spread tile adhesive on tiles.

Paint-mixing container
Make sure you have enough mixed paint for the work, as it is impossible to match colours later.

Safety goggles
These should always be worn when handling powdered materials, such as grout or grout colourant, as well as for cutting tiles.

Tiling a wall with your completed painted tiles can be challenging depending on the size of area you are tiling and the number of tiles that have to be cut. The following tips will help the beginner.

Techniques

Cutting tiles

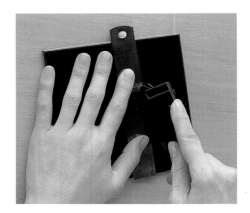

1 To use a hand-held tile cutter, first measure the width required and deduct 2mm/¹⁄₁₆in to allow for grout. Mark the cutting line on the tile. Place the cutting wheel against a short metal ruler and score the line once only to pierce the glaze.

2 Wearing protective leather gloves and safety goggles, place the tile as far as it will go into the jaws of the cutter with the scored line positioned in the centre, then close the handles of the cutter to snap the tile in two.

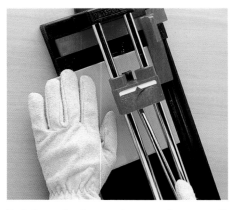

3 Manual tile-cutting machines will cut tiles up to about 5mm/¼in thick quickly and accurately, and they have a useful measuring gauge. Adjust the gauge to the correct width, then pull the wheel once down the tile to score a cutting line. Snap along this line.

4 Wearing protective leather gloves, a face mask and safety goggles, use a tile file to smooth along the cut edge of the tile if desired.

Right: Tile cutters, grout, tiles and a straightedge are just a few of the items you will need to tile an area.

Mixing grout

When colouring grout, mix enough for the whole project, as it is difficult to match the colour in a second batch.

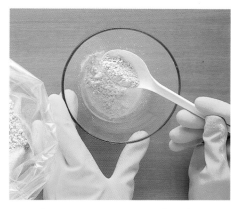

1 When mixing up powdered grout, add the powder to a measured amount of water, rather than the other way round, otherwise the mixture may be lumpy. Mix the powder thoroughly into the water. Always wear rubber (latex) gloves, a protective face mask and goggles.

2 Grout colourant can be added to the powdered grout before mixing it with water. Wear protective clothing as for powdered grout, and then mix with water in the proportion advised by the manufacturer.

Removing grease

You many wish to decorate tiles that are not in pristine condition. It is essential to start with a clean surface to ensure an even application of paint. To remove grease and fingerprints from the surface of tiles before you paint them, wipe with a solution of 1 part malt vinegar to 10 of water.

Below: Single painted tiles can be used to break up a plainly tiled wall.

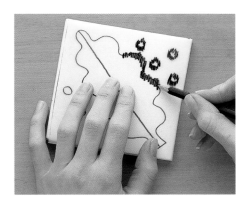

Transferring a design

Cut a piece of tracing paper the same size as the tile. Centre the design, then trace it. Centre the paper design-side down on the tile, matching the edges. Scribble over the lines to transfer to the tile. If the design is not symmetrical, scribble over the lines on to a piece of paper. Place the tracing design-side up on the tile and redraw over the original lines.

Tiling a Wall

It is vital to prepare the surface to be tiled properly so that the tiles will adhere well. And, as with most techniques, the more you practise, the more skilled you will become.

1 To prepare wall surfaces, remove wallpaper or flaking paint, and fill cracks and holes. Leave new plaster to dry for 4 weeks and seal it before tiling. Wash emulsion (latex) paint with sugar soap then sand, wearing a protective face mask, to provide a key (scuffed surface) for the tiles.

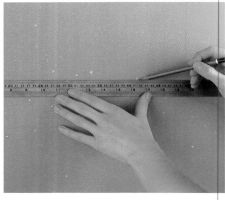

2 It is important to calculate the number of tiles before you begin. Using a long metal ruler or metal tape measure, first find the centre of the wall. You usually need to cut some tiles to fit the wall. Set the cut tiles in the corners or at the edges of walls, where they will be least noticeable.

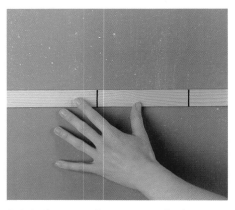

3 Mark a wooden strip with divisions one tile wide plus an extra 2mm/¹⁄₁₆in for grouting either side. Place in the centre of the wall, holding it first vertically, then horizontally. If the edges of the wall fall between two divisions on the strip, you can see the width of the cut tiles needed.

4 Wall tiles are applied upwards from a baseline, usually one tile up from a skirting (base) board, sink or the side of a bath. Draw the baseline, then attach a batten with the top edge along the line. Hammer the nails in part-way, then check with a spirit (carpenter's) level that it is straight.

5 Use a plumbline to establish a true vertical at the side of the batten. Using a set square, draw a second line at this point to mark the side edge of the first complete tile in each row. Attach a batten along the outside of the line, hammering it in place with nails as before.

6 Wearing rubber (latex) gloves, spread a thin layer of tile adhesive (approximately 3mm/⅛in deep) over the wall, inside the battens. Work on a small area at a time, otherwise the adhesive will dry before you have time to tile the wall.

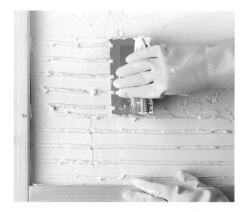

7 Using a notched spreader, "comb" the tile adhesive to provide a key (scuff) to the surface so that the tiles will adhere well. If you do not provide a good surface, the finished result will be less successful.

8 Starting in the bottom corner, position the first tile in place, where the two wooden battens meet. Push it into position with a slight twisting movement of the wrist, to ensure that the back of the tile is completely coated with tile adhesive.

9 Some tiles have built-in spacer lugs. If not, use plastic spacers at the corners of the tiles so that the grouting lines are regular. Remove excess adhesive with a damp sponge before it hardens. As you go, check the tiles with a spirit (carpenter's) level every few rows to make sure they are straight, and adjust as necessary.

10 When the tile adhesive is dry, remove the battens. Add cut tiles at the edges of the tiled areas if necessary. Leave for about 24 hours. Using the rubber edge of the spreader, apply grout to the gaps between the tiles. It is important to use the right type of grout depending on where the tiles are used. Make sure that the gaps are completely filled, or small holes will appear as the grout dries.

11 When the grout has hardened slightly, pull a round-ended stick along the gaps between the tiles to give a smooth finish to the grout. Add a little more grout at this stage if you notice any small holes in the previous layer.

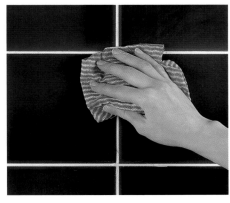

12 Leave the grout to set for about 30 minutes, then remove the excess with a damp sponge. When the grout is completely dry, polish the surface of the tiles with a dry, lint-free cloth to remove any remaining smudges and to give a glossy finish.

These cheerful tiles are based on simple Mexican designs. The motifs are easy to do so you can paint a set quite quickly. They will add a colourful touch to a kitchen wall, as an all-over design or a border.

Mexican Folk Art Tiles

You will need

soft pencil

clean, off-white glazed ceramic tiles

medium and fine paintbrushes

non-toxic, water-based, cold-set

ceramic paints

paint palette

1 Using a soft pencil, draw a simple flower and spotted border design on one of the tiles.

2 Fill in the petals, using a medium paintbrush. Add a dot of contrasting paint for the flower centre.

3 Paint the border in a dark colour, leaving the spots blank. Using a fine paintbrush and various colours, paint a small spot in the centre of each blank spot. Leave to dry.

Children will love these chunky letter tiles. Use them to make a panel or a frieze around a bedroom or playroom wall, mixing the letters at random or spelling out a name. Use non-toxic ceramic paints.

Alphabet Tiles

You will need
fine black felt-tipped pen
clean, plain white glazed ceramic tiles
fine and medium artist's paintbrushes
non-toxic, water-based, cold-set
ceramic paint: black
paint palette

1 Using a fine felt-tipped pen, draw the outline of the letter on to one tile, extending the lines right to the edges of the tile. Using a fine paintbrush, go over the outlines with black paint. Leave to dry.

2 Using a medium paintbrush, paint bold black stripes down one side of the tile, as shown.

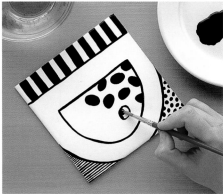

3 Leaving the letter white, fill in the rest of the design with dots, spots and fine lines. Leave to dry thoroughly.

The elegance of Roman numerals is timeless. Assemble these tiles inside a porch and use them to make up a particular date, such as the year your house was built.

Roman Numeral Tiles

You will need
scissors
scrap paper
stencil cardboard
clean, plain white glazed ceramic tiles
metal ruler
pencil
self-healing cutting mat
craft knife
small stencil brush
non-toxic, water-based, cold-set
ceramic paint: blue
spray ceramic varnish

1 Cut a piece of scrap paper and a piece of stencil cardboard the same size as the tile. Using a ruler and pencil, draw the numeral on the scrap paper. Transfer the numeral on to the stencil cardboard.

2 Place the stencil cardboard on a cutting mat. Using a craft knife, carefully cut away the cardboard inside the pencil lines. Place the stencil on the tile, aligning the corners, and stipple blue paint on to the tile. Leave to dry.

3 Working in a well-ventilated area, place the painted tile on a large sheet of scrap paper. Holding the spray can about 30cm/12in from the tile, spray it all over with an even layer of the ceramic varnish.

Trace these jolly designs from the back of the book, outline the shapes in a dark colour, then fill them in with jewel-bright shades. The bold designs are ideal for a child's bathroom.

Cartoon Tiles

You will need

tracing paper

pencil

clean, plain white glazed ceramic tiles

fine artist's paintbrush

non-toxic, water-based, cold-set ceramic paints in various colours

paint palette

1 Trace the motifs provided and transfer to the tile. Using dark green, paint over the outlines. Add spots to the background area. Leave to dry.

2 Colour in the design. Paint spots on the fish. Leave to dry thoroughly.

The details on these tiles are incised into the wet paint in a traditional form of decoration known as sgraffito. Paint a set of tiles one at a time so that the paint does not dry before you add the sgraffito.

Sgraffito Fish Tiles

You will need
chinagraph pencil (optional)
clean, plain white glazed ceramic tiles
tracing paper (optional)
pencil (optional)
non-toxic, water-based, cold-set
ceramic paints: dark blue and
turquoise
medium artist's paintbrushes
paint palette
engraver's scribing tool or sharp pencil
varnish as recommended by the
paint manufacturer

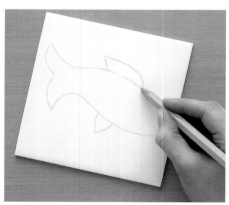

1 Using a chinagraph pencil, draw the outline of the fish on to the tile. Alternatively, enlarge the template from the back of the book and transfer to the tile.

2 Fill in the fish shape with dark blue paint using a medium paintbrush. While the paint is still wet, scratch decorative details on to the fish shape with an engraver's scribing tool or sharp pencil.

3 Fill in the background with turquoise paint, leaving a fine white outline around the fish. Scratch a swirl at each corner, as shown. Leave to dry, then seal the surface with a coat of the recommended varnish.

These deliciously pretty tiles are sponged in two tones of pink, then painted with tiny rosebuds. Sponging is simple and an ordinary bath sponge will suffice, provided it has a well-defined, open texture.

Rosebud Tiles

You will need

non-toxic, water-based, cold-set ceramic paints: pink, white, red and green

paint palette

natural sponge or highly textured nylon sponge

clean, plain white glazed ceramic tiles

medium artist's paintbrush

1 Mix the pink paint with white to give a very pale pink. Dip the sponge in the paint and apply randomly over the tile, leaving white spaces here and there. Leave to dry.

2 Add more pink to the mixed paint to darken it. Sponge this colour over the tile, allowing the first colour to show through. Leave to dry, then sponge a little white paint on top.

3 Using red paint and a paintbrush, paint rosebud shapes randomly on to the sponged tile. Using green paint, add three leaves to each rosebud as shown. Leave to dry thoroughly.

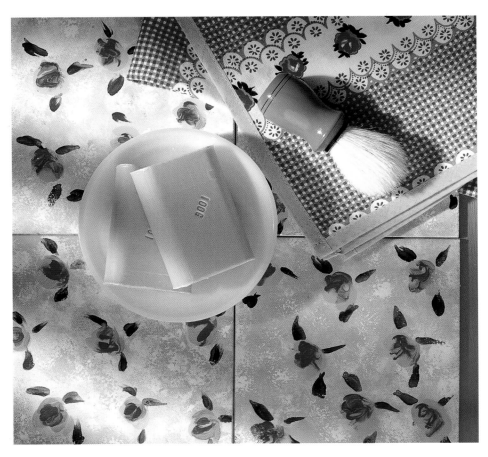

Four plain ceramic tiles combine to make a striking mural, reminiscent of Japanese art in its graphic simplicity and clear, calm blue-and-white colour scheme.

Maritime Tile Mural

You will need

soft and hard pencils

tracing paper

masking tape

4 clean, plain white glazed 15cm/6in square ceramic tiles

chinagraph pencil

non-toxic, water-based, cold-set ceramic paints: mid-blue, dark blue and black

paint palette

small and fine artist's paintbrushes

1 Trace the template from the back of the book and enlarge, if necessary. Tape the tracing to the four tiles, positioning it centrally. Transfer the outline to the tiles with a hard pencil.

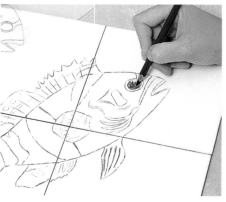

2 Trace over the outline again with a chinagraph pencil. Draw the border freehand, and add any extra details to the fish. Follow the finished picture as a guide.

3 Keep the tiles together as you paint. Using the ceramic paints, fill in the fish shape. First, paint the main part of the fish mid-blue.

4 Paint the detail and the border dark blue. Highlight the scales with black. Set the paint following the manufacturer's instructions. The painted tiles will withstand gentle cleaning.

This quirky cherub tile panel will add cheery individuality to any wall. Decorated in the style of Majolica ware, with bright colours and a stylized design, this romantic cherub is easy to paint.

Cherub Tiles

You will need
pencil
tracing paper
4 clean, plain white, glazed, square
ceramic tiles
fine artist's paintbrushes
non-toxic, water-based, cold-set
ceramic paints: dark blue,
yellow and red
paint palette

1 Trace the template from the back of the book. Enlarge the design on to a piece of tracing paper. Use a pencil to transfer a quarter of the design to each ceramic tile.

2 With a fine brush, and dark blue paint, paint over the main outline on each tile. If required, heat the tiles in the oven for the time specified by the paint manufacturer, to set the outline.

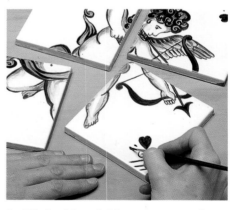

3 Fill in the wings, hair and drapery with yellow paint. Allow the paint to dry. Mix yellow with red to add darker tones, using the finished picture as a guide. Bake the tiles again, to prevent the colours from smudging.

4 With diluted blue paint, mark in the shadows on the cherub's face and body. Go over any areas that need to be defined with more blue paint. Paint the corner motifs freehand and then bake for the final time.

This is a great idea for decorating plain ceramic tiles, which could then be framed and hung on the wall. Alternatively, you could break up a plain white tiled surface with random floral tiles.

Floral Tiles

You will need

clean, plain white glazed ceramic tiles
tracing paper
soft and hard pencils
masking tape
medium and fine artist's paintbrushes
non-toxic, water-based, cold-set
ceramic paints: green, yellow,
red and blue
paint palette and jar

1 Trace the template at the back of the book and enlarge it. Turn the paper over and rub over the outline with a pencil. Tape the transfer to the tile and draw over the outline with a hard pencil to transfer the motif on to the tile.

2 Using a medium paintbrush and thin layers of paint, colour in the leaves and petals. If required, bake in the oven to set the paint, according to the paint manufacturer's instructions.

3 With a fine paintbrush and blue paint, draw in the outline and detail of the petals, leaves and stalk. Paint dots in the centre of the flower. Transfer the corner motifs, and paint them blue with a fine paintbrush. Set the paint by baking the tile. The tile will withstand gentle cleaning.

These Florentine-style tiles are based on ceramic decoration of the Renaissance. A single tile could be a focal point in a bathroom, or you could arrange several together to form interesting repeat patterns.

Italianate Tiles

You will need

clean, plain white glazed square tiles

tracing paper

soft and hard pencils

masking tape

non-toxic, water-based, cold-set ceramic paints: mid-green, dark blue-green, rust-red and dark blue

medium and fine artist's paintbrushes

paint palette

2 Paint the leaf in mid-green paint and allow to dry. You may need to mix colours to achieve the shades you require. Using a dark blue-green, paint over the outline and mark in the leaf veins. Paint a dot in each corner of the tile in the same colour.

3 Paint a border of rust-coloured leaves and a slightly larger leaf in each corner. Paint a curved scroll at both sides of the large leaf in dark blue. When the paint is completely dry, if required, set it in the oven according to the manufacturer's instructions.

1 Wash and dry the tiles thoroughly. Enlarge the template at the back of the book to fit the size of your tiles. Trace the main motif (and also the border if you wish) and rub the back of the tracing with a soft pencil. Position the tracing on each tile, secure with tape, and draw over the outline with a hard pencil.

This delightful vase of flowers is based on a tile design from the Urbino area of northern Italy, where the Majolica style of pottery decoration developed in the 15th century.

Majolica Tiles

You will need

tracing paper

pencil

clean, plain white glazed ceramic tiles

fine artist's paintbrushes

non-toxic, water-based, cold-set ceramic paints: yellow, orange, royal blue, white, light green and dark green

paint palette

water-based acrylic varnish

1 Trace the vase of flowers design from the back of the book, enlarging it if necessary, and transfer it on to the tile. Begin to paint the design with a fine paintbrush, starting with the palest tones of each colour.

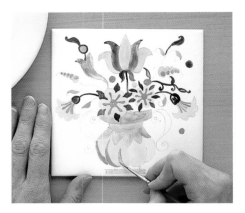

2 Carefully paint in the foliage with light and dark green paint, leaving each colour to dry before applying the next. Add white to orange paint to create a paler shade. Use this to paint the top and bottom of the vase. Using darker orange, fill in the flower centres and emphasize the shape of the vase.

3 Using royal blue paint, outline the shapes of the flowers and vase. Add the vase handles and decorative details to the flowerheads. Leave the tile to dry, then seal the surface with two coats of acrylic varnish, allowing the first coat to dry before applying the second, if required.

Translucent ceramic paints give this exotic tile the rich, glowing colours associated with Byzantine art. The decorative bird motif is taken from a cloisonné enamel panel originally decorated with precious stones.

Byzantine Bird Tile

You will need
tracing paper
pencil
clean, plain white glazed ceramic tile
non-toxic, water-based, cold-set
ceramic paints in a variety of
rich colours
fine artist's paintbrushes
paint palette
gold felt-tipped pen

1 Trace the bird design from the back of the book, enlarging it if necessary, and transfer on to the tile. Paint the bird's head and legs, then start to paint the features, using bright colours.

2 Paint the plants, using your choice of colours. Leave to dry completely.

3 Using a gold felt-tipped pen, draw an outline around every part of the design. As a final touch, add decorative gold details to the bird's feathers and the plants.

The tile-making centre of Puebla in Mexico has been famous for its vibrant, colourful designs since the 17th century. These tiles take their inspiration from the colourful patterns of the Mexican style.

Pueblan Tiles

You will need
pencil
metal ruler
clean, plain white glazed ceramic tiles
non-toxic, water-based, cold-set
ceramic paints:
orange, yellow, royal blue
and turquoise
paint palette
medium artist's paintbrushes

1 Using a pencil and ruler, lightly draw a narrow border around the edge of the tile. Draw a square in all four corners. Paint the borders orange and the squares yellow.

2 Using the same colours, paint a design in the centre of the tile, as shown. Leave to dry completely.

3 Outline the borders and squares in royal blue paint. Then, starting just inside the border at each corner, paint a series of blue arcs, as shown.

4 To decorate the central motif, paint blue circle and diamond shapes over the orange and yellow design, as shown. Add a scalloped edging around the circle and diamond.

5 Using orange paint, paint a small quarter-circle in each corner of the tile to form the repeat. Finally, fill in the background with turquoise paint. Leave to dry completely.

These elegant and highly stylized designs are inspired by the work of Scottish artist Charles Rennie Mackintosh and the Glasgow School of Art at the turn of the 20th century.

Art Nouveau Tiles

You will need

tracing paper

pencil

clean, plain white glazed ceramic tiles

scissors

stencil cardboard

craft knife

self-healing cutting mat

repositionable spray adhesive

large and fine artist's paintbrushes

non-toxic, water-based, cold-set ceramic paints: dark green, light green, deep red and white

paint palette

water-based acrylic varnish

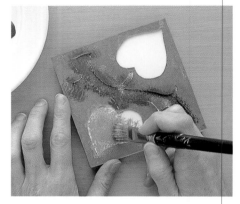

1 Enlarge the designs at the back of the book to fit your tiles. Cut two pieces of stencil cardboard to the size of the tiles and transfer one design to each. Using a craft knife and a cutting mat, cut away the centre of each design. Coat the back of the stencils with adhesive. Place the stem stencil on a tile. Using a dry paintbrush, apply dark green paint to the stems and light green for the leaves.

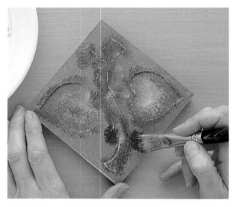

2 Allow the paint to dry completely, then use a clean, dry paintbrush to add a little deep red paint to pick out the thorns on the stem. You might also like to try reversing the stem stencil on some of the tiles, which will make the overall effect more symmetrical.

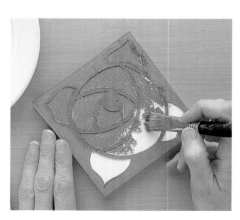

3 Mix deep red paint with white to make a dusky pink shade. Use this colour to stencil the rose motif on to another tile with a dry paintbrush. Leave the paint to dry.

4 Add deep red around the edges of the petals to emphasize the rose shape and give it depth.

5 Using a paintbrush, add a few green dots in the centre of the rose. Leave to dry, then seal the surface of the tiles with two coats of varnish, allowing them to dry between coats, if required.

This cheerful panel is painted freehand across a block of tiles. The paint is applied in several layers, working from light to dark, to give depth and to intensify the colours.

Underwater Panel

You will need
clean, plain white glazed ceramic tiles
soft pencil
non-toxic, water-based, cold-set
ceramic paints: orange, blue, green,
white, red
fine and medium artist's paintbrushes
paint palette

1 Arrange the tiles as close together as possible. Use a soft pencil to sketch your design on the tiles, leaving room around the panel for the border.

2 Starting with the lightest tones of each colour, paint in the fish, shell and seaweed motifs. Allow patches of the white background to show through. Leave to dry.

3 Using medium tones of each colour, loosely paint darker areas to give depth to the sea motifs.

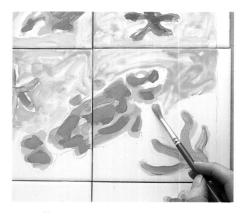

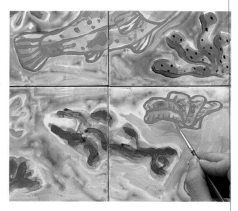

4 Fill in the background sea with diluted blue paint, allowing some of the white to show through.

5 Using a fine paintbrush and a darker tone of each colour, outline the fish, shell and seaweed motifs. Add decorative details, as shown.

6 Using a broad paintbrush, paint a border around the panel. Take the paint over the edges of the tiles where they butt up so there are no ugly gaps. Leave to dry.

This sumptuous and decadent tile is not intended for practical use but to be displayed. The surface is covered with a composite metal leaf, then decorated with a decoupage image photocopied from a book.

Silver Decoupage Tiles

You will need

plain white glazed ceramic tile

cleaning fluid

cloth

water-based Italian size and brush

aluminium composite loose leaf

large, soft brush

purple water-based ink

black and white photocopy

scissors

PVA (white) glue

ceramic tile varnish

1 Clean the tile surface thoroughly to remove any grease. Apply a thin, even coat of size, making sure that the whole surface is covered. Leave it for 15–20 minutes until the size is tacky.

2 Carefully lay the aluminium leaf on the tile. Use a large, dry, soft brush to burnish the aluminium leaf flat and remove any excess.

3 Paint a thin wash of diluted purple ink over the photocopy and leave to dry. Cut out the image. Apply a thin coat of PVA (white) glue to the back and position it on the tile, smoothing the paper down gently in order to remove any air bubbles.

4 Leave the image to dry thoroughly. Seal the surface of the tile with two thin coats of ceramic varnish, allowing the first coat to dry for about 30 minutes before applying the second.

Based on a design by William Morris in 1870, the flowing lines of the flower painting are typical of his bold style. Morris's tiles were often manufactured by designer William de Morgan.

William Morris Tiles

You will need

tracing paper

pencil

4 clean, plain white glazed ceramic tiles

scissors

ballpoint pen

non-toxic, water-based, cold-set ceramic paints: blue, dark green and white

paint palette

medium and fine artist's paintbrushes

1 Enlarge the design from the back of the book so that each square fits on to one tile. Cut it into four separate patterns. Transfer each pattern on to a tile, drawing over the lines with a ballpoint pen.

2 Dilute some of the blue paint, then fill in the two main flower shapes with a medium paintbrush. Leave the paint to dry before proceeding to the next stage.

3 Using undiluted blue paint and a fine paintbrush, work the detailing on the flower petals as shown, to add definition.

4 Using a medium paintbrush, fill in the leaves with dark green paint. The slightly streaky effect that is left by the bristles will add movement to the design. Leave the paint to dry. Highlight the leaves with white veins.

5 Paint green leaves on the flower tiles. Leave to dry, then highlight with white veins as before. Add detailing and fine outlines to the flowers. Leave the tiles to dry completely.

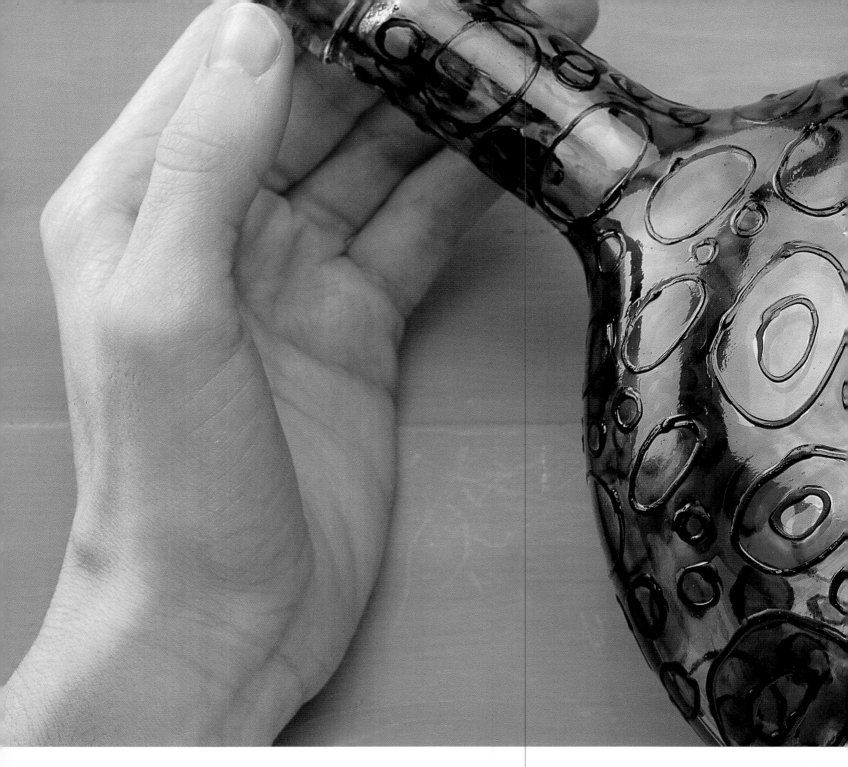

Decorating

Glass

In recent years a wide range of glass paints, in a glorious array of colours, has been made available to the amateur. These paints do not require kiln firing to set the paints, and can be applied easily to glassware. So whether you want to recreate the effect of a stained glass window in your home, or add delicate colour to perfume bottles and champagne flutes to celebrate a special occasion, there are plenty of ideas here to inspire you.

Decorative Details

Glass painting allows you to transform everyday glass bottles, jars, vases, frames, mirrors and even windows into works of art in glorious jewel colours and decorative patterns. All you need are some glass paints, paintbrushes and some glassware to decorate. No specialist skills are required, just a love of colour.

To start with, you can use empty glass bottles and jars salvaged from the kitchen and bathroom to practise on. Then, as you become more proficient and confident, you can progress to decorating plain glass vases, storage jars, perfume bottles, frames,

bowls and even mirrors. You can paint simple dots and squiggles on wine glasses and Christmas baubles, add colourful butterflies and flowers around the outside of glass bowls, decorate jars and frames with charming folk-art

patterns, or perhaps paint trails of pretty flower tendrils across small windows or mirrors.

In addition to painting motifs and patterns, you could try your hand at paint effects on glass, such as sponging, dragging, or scribing with a toothpick.

All of these techniques are clearly explained at the beginning of the chapter, and illustrated with step-by-step instructions.

Contour paste is another element of painting glass. It can be used to outline areas, preventing different colours from merging and blending, or to add raised decorative lines on top of a painted area. Squares of different coloured contour pastes can provide decoration in themselves, without the use of glass paints.

The projects in this chapter feature a variety of different ideas and styles of painting to inspire you, from a colourful glass lantern to brighten an out-

door event, to a frosted vase to add interest to a windowsill. Templates and motifs for many of them can be found at the back of the book, enabling you to transfer the designs exactly. Other projects allow you to experiment with freehand painting, so you can introduce some individual elements into the design. After all, if you make a mistake – you can simply wipe it away.

A variety of materials is needed for painting glass including glass paints and etching paste, available from specialist glass shops, and self-adhesive vinyl, which is available from craft shops.

Materials

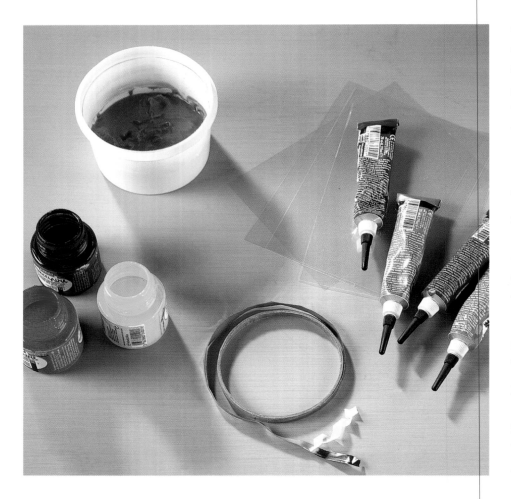

colour. They are not washable, and are designed purely for decorative use. Oil-based and water-based glass paints are available: the two types should not be combined. Ceramic paints can also be used on glass for an opaque effect.

Masking tape

This is ideal for making straight lines for etching and painting.

Paper towels

These are useful for cleaning glass and brushes, and wiping off mistakes.

Reusable adhesive

This is useful for holding designs in place on the glass.

Self-adhesive vinyl

Vinyl is used to mask off large areas when painting and etching the glass.

Acrylic enamel paints

These are ideal for use on glass.

Clear varnish

Mix with glass paints to produce lighter hues.

Contour paste

Use to create raised lines on glass. This gives the look of leaded windows and also acts as a barrier for paints. It can be used to add details within a cell of colour, such as the veins on a leaf.

Epoxy glue

Use this strong, clear glue to attach hanging devices to glass. It takes just a few minutes to go hard.

Etching paste

This acid paste eats into the surface of glass to leave a matt "frosted" finish. Use on clear and pale-coloured glass.

Glass paints

Specially manufactured, glass paints are translucent and give a vibrant

Toothpicks

Use to scratch designs into paintwork.

Ultraviolet glue

This glue goes hard in daylight. Red glass blocks ultraviolet rays, so you should let the light shine through the non-red glass when sticking two colours together, or use epoxy glue.

White spirit (paint thinner)

Use as a solvent to clean off most paints and any errors.

A well-lit workplace and a paintbrush are all that are needed for many of the projects in this chapter. However, the items listed below will make the job easier.

Equipment

Paintbrushes

Use a selection of artist's paintbrushes for applying paint and etching paste. Always clean brushes as directed by the paint manufacturer.

Paint palette

Large quantities of glass paint can be mixed in a plastic ice-cube tray.

Pencils and pens

Use a pencil or dark-coloured felt-tipped pen when making templates. A chinagraph can be used to draw guide-lines on the glass and wipes off easily.

Rubber (latex) gloves

A pair of gloves is vital to protect your hands from etching paste.

Ruler or straightedge

These are essential for measuring, or when a straight line is needed.

Scissors

A pair of small, sharp scissors is useful for various cutting tasks, including cutting out templates.

Sponges

Cut sponges into pieces and use them to apply paint over a large area of glass. A natural sponge can be used to give the paint a decorative mottled effect, whereas a synthetic sponge will give a more regular effect.

Cloth

A piece of cloth or towel folded into a pad is useful to provide support for items such as bottles or bowls while they are being painted. Paint one side of a vessel first, then allow it to dry thoroughly before resting it on the cloth while you paint the rest.

Cotton buds (swabs)

Use these to wipe away any painted mistakes and to remove chinagraph pencil marks.

Craft knife

A craft knife is useful for peeling off contour paste in glass-painting and etching projects. Ensure the blade is sharp and clean.

Nail polish remover

Before painting, always clean the glass on both sides to remove all traces of grease or fingerprints. Household glass cleaning products can be used but nail polish remover is just as good. Use with paper towels.

On the following pages you will find useful step-by-step descriptions of some of the basic glass-painting techniques. They will help you to perfect your skills and achieve beautiful and successful results.

Techniques

Preparing the glass

It is essential to clean the surface of the glass thoroughly to remove any traces of grease or fingermarks, before beginning glass painting.

Clean both sides of the glass thoroughly, using a glass cleaner or nail polish remover and a paper towel.

Using templates and stencils

There are many different templates and stencils suitable for using on glass. Choose the type that is most useful for the size and style of glassware you are decorating.

1 If you are working on a flat piece of clear glass, a template can simply be taped to the underside or attached using pieces of reusable putty adhesive, to ensure it does not move.

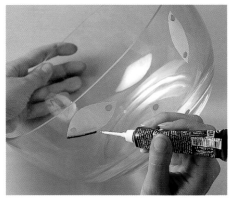

2 When you are decorating a curved surface, such as a bowl, small paper templates can be attached to the inside, following the curve. Use adhesive tape.

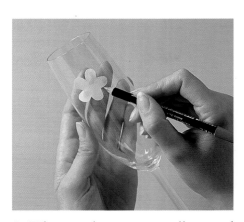

3 When working on a small, curved surface, such as a drinking glass, it may be easier to apply the template to the outside and then draw around it using a chinagraph pencil to make a guide.

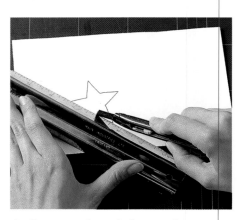

4 Cut straight-sided stencils using a craft knife and metal ruler and resting on a cutting mat. Always keep your fingers well away from the blade and change the blade frequently to avoid tearing the paper.

5 When you are cutting a stencil that includes tight curves, cut what you can with a craft knife, then use a small pair of sharp-pointed scissors to cut the curves smoothly.

Transferring a design

In addition to using templates and stencils, there are several other ways of transferring a design on to glass. You can trace it, sketch with a pen, use carbon paper or even use water.

Using contour paste

Contour paste is easy to use, but it takes a little practice to get the pressure right. As it is the basis of much glass painting, it is worth persevering.

Tracing through the glass

Stick the design in position on the back of the article you wish to transfer it to with reusable putty adhesive or masking tape. For curved vessels cut the design into sections. Trace the design directly on to the surface of the vessel with the tube of contour paste.

Felt-tipped pens

A water-based overhead-projection pen is ideal for sketching freehand on to glass. Many felt-tipped pens will also work. When you are happy with your design, apply contour paste over the lines.

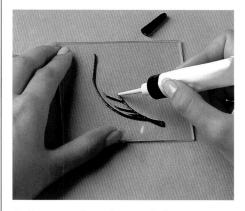

1 Squeeze the tube until the paste just begins to come out, then stop. To draw a line, hold the tube at about 45° to the surface. Rest the tip of the tube on the glass and squeeze it gently while moving the tube.

Water-level technique

To draw even lines around a vase, bowl, or other circular vessel, fill with water to the height of the line. Turn the vessel slowly while tracing the waterline on to the surface of the glass with contour paste.

Using carbon paper

Place a sheet of carbon paper over the article and then the design on top. With a ballpoint pen, trace over the lines of your design, pressing it fairly firmly. Some carbon papers will not work on glass – handwriting carbon paper is the most suitable.

2 Occasionally air bubbles occur inside the tube. These can cause the paste to "explode" out of the tube. If this happens, either wipe off the excess paste straight away with a paper towel, or wait until it has dried and use a craft knife to remove it.

Mixing and applying paint

Glass paints come in a range of exciting, vivid colours, and produce beautiful translucent effects. Practise painting first on a spare piece of glass to get used to the consistency of the paint.

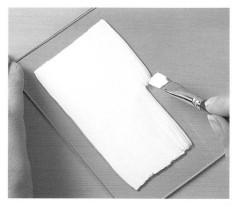

1 Mix paint colours on a ceramic palette, old plate or tile. To make a light colour, add the colour to white or colourless paint, a tiny amount at a time, until you reach the required hue. Use a separate brush for each colour so that you do not contaminate the paint in the pot.

2 If you want the finished effect to be opaque rather than translucent, add a small amount of white glass paint to the transparent coloured paint on the palette, plate or tile.

3 Always use an appropriately sized paintbrush for the job. A large, flat brush will give a smooth and even coverage over larger areas of glass, as well as making the job quicker.

4 Use a very fine brush to paint small details and fine lines. Let one coat of paint dry before painting over it with another colour.

5 To etch a design into the paint, draw into the paint while it is still wet using a toothpick or the other end of the paintbrush. Wipe off the excess paint after each stroke to keep the design clean.

Applying paint with a sponge

Sponging produces a mottled, softened effect on glass surfaces. Experiment first on scrap paper.

1 Use a dampened natural sponge to achieve a mottled effect. Dip the sponge in the paint then blot it on a sheet of paper to remove the excess paint before applying it to the glass.

2 Use masking tape or small pieces of reusable putty adhesive to attach the stencil to the glass for sponging.

3 Add texture and interest to sponged decoration by adding a second colour when the first has dried. This is most effective when both sides of the glass will be visible.

4 Sponge a neat, decorative band around a drinking glass by masking off both sides of the band with strips of masking tape.

Free-styling

Rather than using contour paste to define individual cells of colour, apply a coat of varnish over the article and brush or drop colours into the varnish, allowing them to blend freely.

Flash drying with candles

It is possible to flash dry paintwork over a heat source. A candle is ideal, but take care not to burn yourself. Turn the article slowly about 15cm/ 6in above the flame.

Correcting mistakes

If you don't get your design right first time, it doesn't matter with glass painting. All you need is a cotton bud (swab) or a paper towel and you can simply wipe off the paint before it dries.

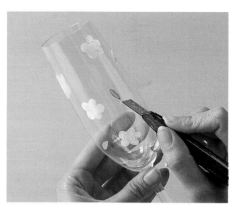

1 Use a cotton bud (swab) to remove a small mistake. Work while the paint is still wet.

2 To remove a larger area of paint, wipe it away immediately using a damp paper towel. If the paint has begun to dry, use nail polish remover.

3 If the paint has hardened completely, small mistakes can be corrected by scraping the paint away using a craft knife.

Etching glass

This technique is easy but very effective and produces a quick, stylish finish. Etch simple shapes such as flowers or leaves for the best results.

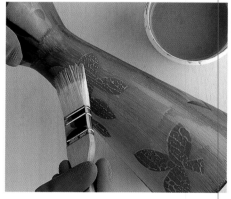

1 Self-adhesive vinyl makes a good mask when etching. Cut out shapes from self-adhesive vinyl. Decide where you want to position them on the glass, remove the backing paper and stick down.

2 Wearing rubber (latex) gloves, paint the etching paste evenly over the glass with a paintbrush. Make sure you do not spread it too thinly, or you will find the effect quite faint. Leave to dry for 3 minutes.

3 Still wearing the rubber gloves, wash the paste off with running water. Then wipe off any residue and rinse. Peel off the shapes and wash again. Dry the glass thoroughly with a clean cotton rag.

For this year's Christmas tree, buy plain glass baubles and decorate them yourself with coloured glass paints to make beautiful, completely original ornaments.

Christmas Baubles

You will need
clean, clear glass baubles
self-adhesive spots
glass etching medium
paper clips
gold contour paste
fine glitter
scrap paper
bright yellow glass paint
fine artist's paintbrush

1 Stick self-adhesive spots all over the baubles. Spray on an even coat of glass etching medium. Hang up each bauble to dry using paper clips.

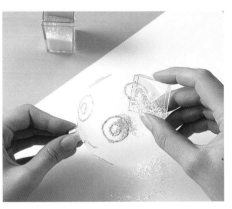

2 Peel off the paper spots to reveal clear circles all over each bauble. Outline each circle with gold contour paste, then draw a second circle around the first. Add some squiggly lines radiating from the neck of the bauble. While the contour paste is still wet, sprinkle it with glitter, holding the bauble over a sheet of paper to catch the excess. Hang the bauble up to dry.

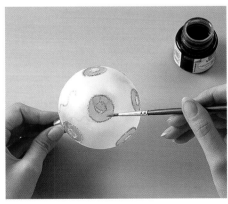

3 Fill in between the inner and outer gold circles with glass paint in bright yellow, and hang the bauble up to dry, using paper clips as before. Repeat for any remaining baubles.

Craft suppliers stock a range of glassware especially for painting, and these small glass hearts would look beautiful catching the light as they twirl in a window.

Heart Decoration

You will need
clean, clear glass heart shapes
nail polish remover or glass cleaner
paper towels
etching paste
medium artist's paintbrush
sponge
contour paste: light gold, dark gold
and bronze

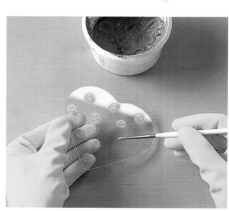

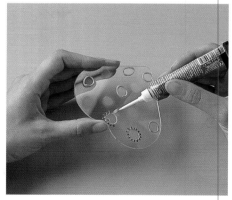

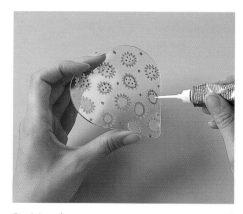

1 Clean both sides of the glass shapes to remove grease. Paint etching paste in small circles all over one side of the glass. Leave to dry, then wash off the paste with warm water and a sponge.

2 Outline alternate etched circles using light gold contour paste. Leave to dry. Add short "rays" all round each outline using dark gold contour paste, then add rays in light gold. Leave the contour paste to dry.

3 Use bronze contour paste to add a few dots between the circles. Turn the heart over and cover the etched areas in dots of bronze contour paste. Leave to dry. Bake the glass to harden the paint if necessary, following the manufacturer's instructions.

Transform plain, everyday glasses with patterns of gold relief outliner. Add clear, stained-glass colours for a jewelled effect and you will give your festive dinner the air of a medieval feast.

Festive Wine Glasses

You will need

plain wine glasses

clean cloths

cleaning fluid

gold contour paste

oil-based glass paints

fine artist's paintbrush

old glass or jar

paper towel

1 Wash the glasses and wipe over with cleaning fluid to remove all traces of grease.

2 Pipe your design directly on to the glass with gold contour paste. Leave to dry thoroughly for at least 24 hours.

3 Check the colour and get the feel of the glass paint, which is rather viscous, by practising on an old glass or jar first. Use a fine paintbrush to colour in your design, and be careful not to get paint on the gold contour paste. Try to finish with each colour before changing to the next one. Clean the brush between each colour.

Create a conversation piece at mealtimes with these contemporary salt and pepper pots, which have been simply decorated with circles, squares and dots in a variety of bright colours.

Painted Salt and Pepper Pots

You will need

clean glass salt and pepper pots
contour paste: black and gold
glass paints in various colours
medium artist's paintbrushes
clear varnish

1 Draw a few loose circles on to the pots with black contour paste.

2 When the lines are dry, colour in the background with glass paint.

3 Fill in the circles with a different coloured paint from the one used for the background. If you prefer, use a variety of different colours.

4 Apply dots of black contour paste over the background colour to add texture to the design.

5 When dry, paint squares over the circles using the gold contour paste. Leave to dry, then paint with clear varnish. Allow to dry.

The decoration on this double-layered glass frame has been painted on to the inside of the glass. This means that you need to paint the details on the leaves first, and the background colour second.

Leaf Photograph Frame

You will need
tracing paper
double-layer glass clip-frame, with cleaned glass
scissors
masking tape
photograph
felt-tipped pen
nail polish remover or glass cleaner
paper towels
fine and medium artist's paintbrushes
glass paints: dark green, light green and pale blue

1 Cut a piece of tracing paper the same size as the frame. Using small tabs of masking tape, stick your chosen photograph in place and mark its position, then draw a selection of leaves around it, following the leaf templates at the back of the book.

2 Thoroughly clean the glass that forms the front of the frame. Remove the photograph and turn the tracing paper back to front. Attach it to the glass using small pieces of masking tape, as shown.

3 Using a fine paintbrush, fill in the leaf stems of the design with the dark green paint. Again using the dark green paint, fill in the small triangle shapes that represent the veins in the leaves. Leave the dark green paint to dry completely.

4 Paint the leaf shapes in light green. Leave the light green paint to dry, then paint the background colour in pale blue. Leave to dry. Remove the template. Bake the glass frame to harden the paint, if necessary. Follow the manufacturer's instructions.

5 Attach your chosen photograph to the second glass sheet, checking its position against the marks on the template. Assemble the frame.

Ordinary glass jars make useful windproof containers for candles to light the garden during summer evenings; using glass paints, you can turn them into magical lanterns.

Glass Lantern

You will need

glass jar
nail polish remover or glass cleaner
paper towels
black relief outliner
tape measure
chinagraph pencil (china marker)
tape reel
glass paints: red and orange
medium and fine paintbrushes
toothpick (optional)
fine wire
wire cutters
8 beads
round-nosed pliers

1 Clean the outside of the glass jar carefully to remove traces of grease and fingermarks, then stand it upside down and draw all around the base using the black relief outliner.

2 Measure 2cm/¾in up from the base of the glass and mark this level using a chinagraph pencil (china marker). Use the outliner to draw a horizontal line around the jar following the reference mark. Draw two more horizontal lines at 2cm/¾in intervals.

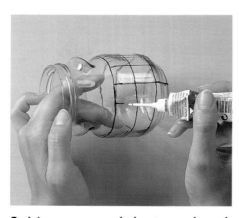

3 Measure around the jar and mark 2cm/¾in intervals with the chinagraph pencil. Referring to these marks, draw vertical lines with the outliner to divide the rings into squares. Leave to dry thoroughly.

4 Support the jar on its side on a tape reel to stop it from rolling around as you work. Paint one of the squares with red paint. Using the end of a fine paintbrush or a toothpick, etch a small star through the centre of the red square. Wipe the paint off the brush after each stroke.

5 Paint the next square orange and etch a star as before. Paint and decorate all the squares, alternating the colours. Work only on the uppermost area so that the paint does not run, and wait for the paint to dry before turning the jar to continue. Bake the glass to harden the paint as required.

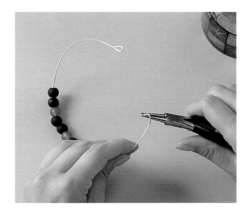

6 Cut a 30cm/12in length of wire and thread the beads on to it. Use a pair of round-nosed pliers to bend each end of the wire into a small loop.

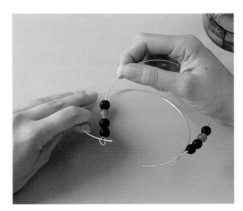

7 Cut a second wire 3cm/1¼in longer than the circumference of the jar. Thread it through the loops in the handle and wrap it around the jar.

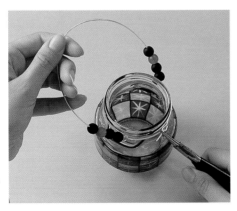

8 Bend one wire end into a loop and and thread the other end through it. Pull it tight, then bend it back and squeeze the hooks closed.

Stained glass is made for sunlight, and this sunlight catcher can hang in any window to catch all of the available light. Gold outliner separates the brightly coloured areas of orange, yellow, red and blue.

Sunlight Catcher

You will need

clean, 20cm/8in diameter clear glass roundel, 4mm/³⁄₁₆in thick

paper

pencil

tracing paper

indelible black felt-tipped pen

gold contour paste

glass paints: orange, yellow, red and blue

fine artist's paintbrush

73cm/29in length of chain

pliers

epoxy glue

1 To make a template of the sun motif that will fit the glass roundel, start by using a pencil to draw around the rim of the roundel on to a piece of paper.

2 Trace the sun motif template from the back of the book and transfer it to the plain paper, enlarging to the size required.

3 Place the circle of glass over the template and trace the design on to the glass using a felt-tipped pen.

4 Trace over the black lines using gold contour paste. Leave to dry.

5 Colour in the central sun motif using the orange and yellow glass paints. Leave to dry. Clean the brush between colours as recommended by the paint manufacturer.

6 Fill in the rest of the design using red and blue glass paints. Leave to dry.

7 Wrap the length of chain around the edge of the glass and cut to size. Rejoin the links by squeezing firmly together with pliers.

8 Cut an 8cm/3¼in length of chain, open the links at each end, and attach it to the chain circle by squeezing with pliers. Glue the chain circle around the circumference of the glass roundel using epoxy glue.

Get into the spirit of summer with this unusual etched lemonade pitcher. Etching is particularly suitable for eating or drinking vessels as once the piece has been washed, there is no surface residue.

Lemonade Pitcher

You will need

clean glass pitcher

tape measure

tracing paper

pencil

scissors

reusable putty adhesive

black contour paste

self-adhesive vinyl or PVA (white) glue
and brush

etching paste

1cm/½in decorator's paintbrush

washing up (dishwashing) brush

craft knife

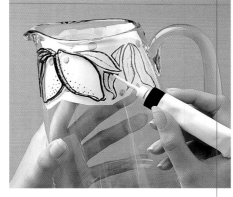

1 Measure the top rim of the pitcher. Trace and enlarge the template at the back of the book to fit. Cut into sections and space evenly inside the pitcher, just below the neck. Trace the design on to the glass with the contour paste. Leave to dry for 2 hours.

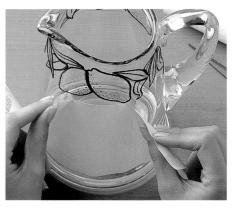

2 Cover all of the pitcher (except the design area) with self-adhesive vinyl or two costs of PVA (white) glue. If using glue, leave the first coat to dry completely before applying the next.

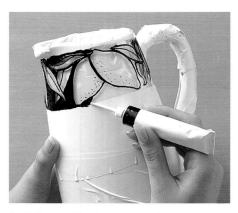

3 Fill in all of the gaps between the outlines of the lemons and leaves and the vinyl (or glue) with black contour paste. Apply the etching paste with the decorator's paintbrush following the manufacturer's instructions.

4 Wash off the etching paste with cold water. If the etching paste has done its job, the glass should now be evenly etched without clear patches or streaks, but if it does not seem quite right, reapply the etching paste.

5 Carefully lift the edge of the contour paste with a craft knife. Peel off the vinyl (if used) and the contour paste. The paste will peel off more easily if you warm the pitcher by wrapping it in a hot towel first.

This picture frame is simply decorated using a gold marker and glass paints. The design is inspired by the devotional art and the remarkable patterns that adorn the Alhambra Palace in Granada, southern Spain.

Alhambra Picture Frame

You will need
clip-frame, with cleaned glass
gold permanent felt-tipped pen
fine artist's paintbrush
glass paints: crimson, turquoise and
deep blue
piece of glass
scissors
kitchen sponge
paper towel

1 Enlarge the template at the back of the book to fit the clip-frame. Remove the glass from the frame and place it over the design. Trace it on to the glass with a gold permanent felt-tipped pen.

2 Turn the sheet of glass over. Using a fine paintbrush, paint over the diamond shapes with the crimson glass paints. Leave a white border between the crimson and the gold outline.

3 Pour a little turquoise and a little deep blue paint on to a piece of glass. Cut a kitchen sponge into sections. Press the sponge into the paint and then apply it to the glass with a light, dabbing motion to colour in the border. Clean up any overspill with a paper towel and leave to dry.

This is a magical way to transform a plain glass vase into something stylish and utterly original. When you have etched the vase, make sure that it is evenly frosted before you peel off the leaves.

Frosted Vase

You will need
coloured glass vase
tracing paper
pencil
thin cardboard or paper
scissors
self-adhesive vinyl
etching paste
medium artist's paintbrush

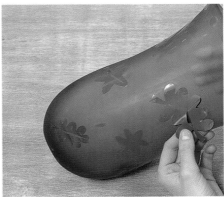

1 Wash and dry the vase. Draw a leaf pattern, then trace it on to a piece of thin cardboard or paper. Cut them out. Draw around the templates on to the backing of the vinyl and draw small circles freehand.

2 Cut out the shapes and peel off the backing paper. Arrange the shapes all over the vase. Smooth them down carefully to avoid any wrinkles. Paint etching paste over the vase and leave it in a warm place to dry, following the manufacturer's instructions.

3 Wash the vase in warm water to remove the paste. If the frosting looks smooth, you can remove the shapes. If not, repeat the process with another coat of etching paste, then wash and remove the shapes.

Decorate a glass storage jar with frosting and coloured glass paints. The frosted-look background is etched first and the flowers are painted in afterwards using a selection of brightly coloured glass paints.

Kitchen Storage Jar

You will need

clean glass storage jar

self-adhesive vinyl

felt-tipped pen

small, sharp scissors

etching paste

medium artist's paintbrushes

clean cotton rag

washing-up liquid

(dishwashing detergent)

glass paints in various colours

clear varnish

1 Decide on an overall pattern for the storage jar and draw the design on to a piece of self-adhesive vinyl with a felt-tipped pen.

2 Cut out the individual shapes from the self-adhesive vinyl carefully using small, sharp scissors.

3 Position all the adhesive shapes on to the outside of the storage jar and lid in an even design and press them down firmly.

4 Brush a thick and even layer of etching paste over both the jar and lid. Leave to dry completely.

5 Wash the storage jar and lid thoroughly and then wipe them dry using a clean cotton rag.

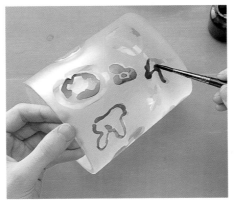

6 Peel off the plastic shapes once the shapes are etched deeply enough.

7 Remove the remains of the plastic with washing-up liquid (dishwashing detergent) and a clean cotton rag. Paint in the shapes with glass paints.

8 Leave to dry, then varnish the painted areas only with clear varnish. When the jar is completely dry, fill as desired.

This jazzy painted bottle will really brighten up a bathroom shelf. It is decorated with a fun bubble pattern in blues and greens, but you can experiment with designs to complement the shape of your bottle.

Patterned Bathroom Bottle

You will need

clean glass bottle with a cork

felt-tipped pen

paper

black contour paste

glass paints: blue, green, violet and turquoise

fine artist's paintbrushes

turquoise glass nugget

ultraviolet glue

bubble bath

1 Decide on the pattern you think would look best for your bottle, then sketch your design to scale on a piece of paper.

2 Wash and thoroughly dry the bottle you have chosen. Then, using a felt-tipped pen, copy your design carefully on to the bottle.

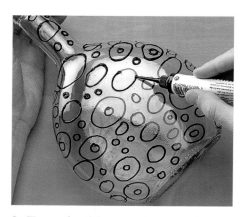

3 Trace the felt-tipped pen design on one side of the bottle with the black contour paste. Leave the contour paste to dry completely.

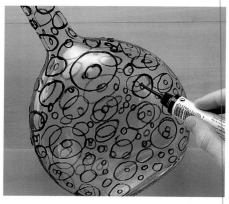

4 Turn the bottle over and add contour paste circles to the other side. Leave to dry as before.

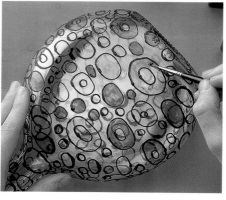

5 When the contour paste is dry, paint inside the circle motifs using blue, green and violet glass paints. Clean all the paintbrushes thoroughly between colours, as recommended by the paint manufacturer.

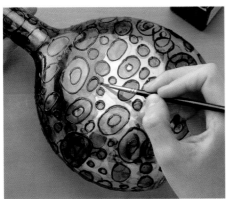

6 Once the circles are dry, paint the surrounding area using turquoise glass paint. Leave to dry.

7 Using ultraviolet glue, stick a glass nugget to the top of the cork.

8 Fill the bottle with your favourite bubble bath and replace the cork.

Celebratory champagne bubbles were the inspiration for these gold-spotted glasses. A fine mist of white paint is applied with a sponge. This is accentuated with a raised design of gold bubbles.

Champagne Flutes

You will need

clean, clear glass champagne flutes

nail polish remover or glass cleaner

paper towels

flat paintbrush

white glass paint

ceramic tile or old plate

natural sponge

water or white spirit (paint thinner)

scrap paper

felt-tipped pen

gold contour paste

1 Clean the champagne glasses carefully to remove any traces of grease and fingermarks. Using a flat paintbrush, apply a thin film of white glass paint over the surface of a ceramic tile or an old plate.

2 Moisten a piece of natural sponge, using water if the glass paint is water-based or white spirit (paint thinner) if it is oil-based. Dab the sponge on to the paint on the tile or plate.

3 Sponge white paint lightly on to the base, the stem and the lower part of the bowl of each champagne flute. Leave to dry thoroughly. Draw around the base of one glass on a small piece of scrap paper to make a template.

4 Fold the template into eighths, open it out and draw along the fold lines with a pen. Stand the glass on the template and dot along the guide-lines using a gold contour paste. Add dots in a gradual spiral around the glass stem, turning the glass slowly and working upwards.

5 Add more dots on the bowl of the glass, making the dots smaller and placing them further apart as you work up the glass. Place the final dots 2.5cm/1in below the rim so that they do not come in contact with the lips. Repeat with the other glasses. Set the paint following the paint manufacturer's instructions.

A flurry of butterflies and flowers covers the surface of this stunning bowl. They are painted freehand, with a few brush strokes forming each wing or petal, and the details are etched into the wet paint.

Butterfly Bowl

You will need
clear glass bowl
nail polish remover or glass cleaner
paper towels
tape measure
chinagraph pencil
rounded medium and fine paintbrushes
glass paints: grey, violet, mauve, bright pink, pale blue and jade green
toothpick
cotton buds (swabs)

1 Clean the bowl. Measure 5.5cm/2¼in down from the rim and mark the edge of the border with a chinagraph pencil. Divide the border into equal sections, 5.5cm/2¼in wide.

2 To paint a butterfly just below the border, use a rounded paintbrush for the body and apply a single brush stroke in grey paint. Use a fine paintbrush to paint the antennae.

3 Using violet paint, paint a pair of wings on each side of the body. While the paint is still wet, use a toothpick to etch a simple design on the wings. Paint butterflies at random all over the bowl below the border, using mauve paint for some of the wings.

4 To paint the flowers for the border area, start with the centres. Paint a small circle in the middle of each of the measured sections with the mauve glass paint.

5 Use the medium paintbrush to paint five petals radiating out from one mauve flower centre, using the bright pink glass paint. Proceed to the next step before adding the remaining flower petals.

6 Etch a line along each petal, using a toothpick. Paint the rest of the petals and leave to dry.

7 Below the border, fill in the areas between the butterflies with swirls of pale blue paint. Leave to dry.

8 Rub off the pencil with cotton buds (swabs). Paint waves between the flowers using jade. Set the paint.

Cheap clip-frames are widely available in almost any size you need. This one is decorated with contour paste in a range of colours which have been dragged together while still wet to create an intricate design.

Geometric Bordered Frame

You will need
clip-frame
scrap paper
felt-tipped pen
ruler
nail polish remover or glass cleaner
paper towels
reusable putty adhesive
contour paste: yellow, bright pink,
green and orange
toothpick

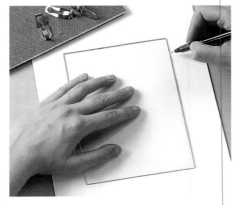

1 Dismantle the frame and place the glass on a sheet of scrap paper. Draw around the edge of the glass.

2 Divide the marked edge equally and draw a double border of squares around the template.

3 Clean the glass thoroughly to remove any traces of grease. Attach the cleaned glass to the paper template with a small piece of reusable putty adhesive at each of the corners.

4 Using yellow contour paste, trace around the first square very carefully, drawing just inside the guidelines of the paper template.

5 Using the bright pink contour paste, draw a slightly smaller square just inside the yellow one. Make sure the two colours meet up exactly without any gap.

6 Draw a third line in the same way using green contour paste. Draw carefully to avoid smudging the yellow and pink paste.

7 Fill the centre of the square with the orange contour paste. Work in single strokes to prevent the orange and green paints from blending.

8 Working while the paste is still wet, use a toothpick to drag the colours from the corners of the square into the centre. Clean the excess paint from the toothpick with a paper towel after each stroke to keep the design neat.

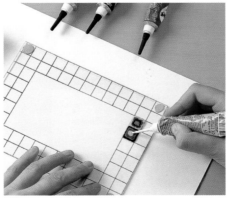

9 Drag another line from the middle of each side of the square into the centre. Wipe the toothpick after each stroke. Repeat on the next square: this time start with green, then use orange, pink and finally yellow in the centre.

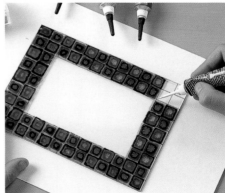

10 Work all around the border of the frame, alternating the combinations of colours. Leave the frame to dry completely. Bake the glass to harden the paint, if necessary, following the manufacturer's instructions.

Filled with water and floating candles, this bowl becomes a magical item. Set it on the dining table with the bowl as a centrepiece, or place it in the bathroom, fill the bath, sit back and relax.

Lily Candle Bowl

You will need

masking tape

clean glass bowl

tracing paper

felt-tipped pen

scissors

reusable putty adhesive

black contour paste

glass paints: emerald, deep blue, turquoise, yellow and white

clear varnish

paint palette

fine artist's paintbrushes

piece of glass

washing-up (dishwashing) sponge

cotton buds (swabs)

white spirit (paint thinner)

craft knife

1 Stick masking tape around the rim of the bowl. Trace the template from the back of the book, enlarge it and cut it into small sections. Attach it to the inside of the bowl with reusable putty adhesive. On the outside of the bowl, trace over the design with black contour paste. Complete one half of the bowl, leave it to dry, then do the other half. Draw wavy lines with black contour paste across the bowl between the lily-pads. Leave to dry.

2 Mix one part of emerald glass paint with one part varnish in a container. Repeat with the blue, turquoise and yellow paints. Use a brush to transfer the paint on to a piece of glass. Cut a washing-up (dishwashing) sponge into sections, one piece for each colour. Place the bowl upside down and sponge the turquoise and deep blue over the background. Then sponge emerald and yellow over each lily-pad. Leave to dry for 1–2 hours.

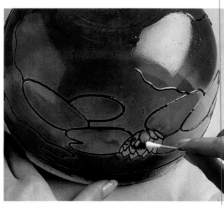

3 Dip a cotton bud (swab) in white spirit (paint thinner) and use it to clean the coloured paint from the flower petals.

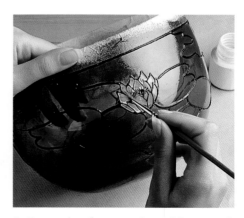

4 Paint the flowers white. Use a craft knife to peel off the contour paste from around the lily-pads, leaving the paste around the flowers intact.

Stems of French lavender, with their picturesque winged flowerheads, criss-cross over the front of this beautiful vase. Opaque paints give the flowers solidity and impact against the clear glass.

French-lavender Flower Vase

You will need
tracing paper
felt-tipped pen
straight-sided glass vase
scissors
masking tape
nail polish remover or glass cleaner
paper towels
high-density synthetic sponge
opaque ceramic paints: gold, white, purple, crimson and green
paint palette
medium and fine artist's paintbrushes

1 Trace the template at the back of the book, enlarging it as necessary to fit the vase. Using masking tape, attach the tracing to the inside of the glass. Clean the outside of the vase thoroughly to remove any traces of grease and fingermarks.

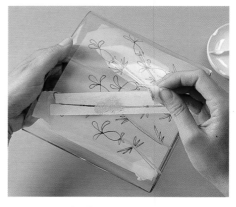

2 Draw a shallow curve along a length of masking tape and cut along it. Stick the two parts to the vase, following one of the stems on the template and leaving a 3mm/⅛in space between them. Sponge gold paint along the stem and leave to dry. Peel off the tape and repeat for the other stems.

3 Mix white with purple paint and fill in the teardrop shapes for the flower-heads in light purple. Add darker shades of purple and crimson towards the bottom end of each flower shape, stippling the paint to create texture.

4 Paint the three petals at the top of each flower in pale purple, using long, loose brush strokes. Leave the paint to dry. Indicate the individual florets on each flowerhead with small ovals in dark purple. Leave the paint to dry.

5 Using a fine paintbrush, draw spiky leaves along the stems in two or three shades of dusky green. Leave to dry completely, and then bake the vase to harden the paint if necessary, following the manufacturer's instructions.

Some bottles are too beautiful to discard. This elegantly shaped blue one has been recycled with a decoration inspired by a 19th-century original found in an antique shop.

Bohemian Bottle

You will need
tracing paper
pencil
scissors
blue bottle
nail polish remover or glass cleaner
paper towels
masking tape
chinagraph pencil
ceramic paints: gold, white, green, red and yellow
medium and fine artist's paintbrushes
paint palette

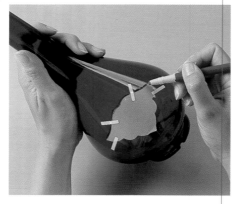

1 Trace the template at the back of the book and cut out the bold centre section. Clean the bottle to remove any grease and fingermarks. Tape the template to the bottle and draw all around it using a chinagraph pencil.

2 Fill in the shape with several coats of gold paint, stippling it on to create a textured effect. Leave the paint to dry. Using white paint and a fine brush, outline the shape and add swirls along the top edge.

3 Mix white with a little green paint and shade the border design with touches of pale green.

4 Paint the green leaves with loose brush strokes, and add highlights in pale green. Draw in the red and yellow dots along the curves of the border as well as for the flower centres.

5 Paint in the daisy petals around the red flower centres using white paint. Add three small hearts and one or two small yellow flowers to the design for decorative detail.

Painted glassware was a popular folk art form in Europe, with bright figures used to adorn glass, wood, fabric and ceramics. Try to find old glasses in junk or antique shops to decorate.

Folk Art Glass

You will need

tape measure

tall glass

scissors

tracing paper

pencil

masking tape (optional)

soft cloth

enamel paint thinners

enamel paints: red, green, yellow, blue, black and white

fine artist's paintbrushes

elastic band

1 Measure around your glass, top and bottom, and cut a piece of tracing paper to fit in it. Trace the template from the back of the book and put the tracing into the glass, using the masking tape to secure it, if necessary.

2 Rest the glass on a cloth. Support your painting hand with your other hand. The enamel paint should be thinned just enough to flow nicely and be slightly transparent. Use light strokes and avoid overpainting.

3 Add small dots and motifs to suit your glass; if you have a fluted base, emphasize this with a pattern. Allow one side of the glass to dry first before painting the other, unless you support the glass on its rim by splaying your other hand inside the glass.

4 When the paint has dried, place an elastic band around the glass to act as a guide, and then paint stripes of colour around it, as shown. Support the glass with a cloth and your other hand, as described in step 2.

5 Finally, introduce some individual touches by adding embellishments of your own to the design, perhaps in the form of just a few squiggles, some dots or even your initials.

This enchanting perfume bottle, with its swags of little dots and pretty little gilded flowers, is reminiscent of 19th-century Italian enamelled glassware. Use opaque ceramic paints for this project.

Venetian Perfume Bottle

You will need

round clear glass bottle with stopper

nail polish remover or glass cleaner

paper towels

tracing paper

pencil

scrap paper

scissors

chinagraph pencil

opaque ceramic paints: white,

red and gold

fine artist's paintbrush

paint palette

cotton buds (swabs)

1 Clean the bottle. Trace the template at the back of the book, adjusting it to fit eight times around the bottle, then cut out the scallops.

4 Using the template design as a guide, paint a four-petalled flower in gold paint between each scallop in the first round. Then fill in the centres of the daisies in gold paint.

2 Use a chinagraph pencil to draw around scallop A eight times, fitting it close to the neck of the bottle. Draw in the curls, then draw around scallop B, fitting it between the first scallops.

5 Using the fine paintbrush, add tiny dots of white, gold and pink paint in delicate swags and lines to link the flowers. Fill in the gold ovals, and pink and white dots at the top of each heart, then complete the design with two small gold dots at the base of each pink daisy. Extend the design with rows of tiny dots up the neck of the perfume bottle.

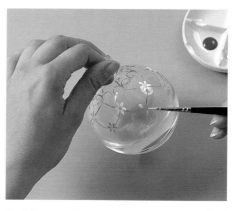

3 Using white, paint a six-petalled daisy at the base of each upper scallop. Mix a little red paint with white, and paint eight pink daisies at the base of each lower scallop.

6 Paint a large pink daisy exactly in the centre of the bottle stopper and add a gold centre to the daisy shape, as well as rows of tiny white dots radiating from the petals. Leave the paint to dry completely, then rub off the pencil marks using a cotton bud (swab). Bake the bottle and stopper to harden the paint, if necesary, following the manufacturer's instructions.

This cabinet uses opaque enamels rather than transparent glass paints, in the tradition of Eastern European folk art. Folk art relies on basic colour combinations and simple brushwork.

Folk Art Cabinet

You will need

small, glass-fronted display cabinet

reusable putty adhesive

fine artist's paintbrush

acrylic enamel paints: white, light green, deep green, red, raw sienna, yellow

paint palette

1 Enlarge the template from the back of the book and stick it to the back of the glass door with reusable putty adhesive. Paint the design on to the front of the glass using white acrylic enamel paint. Leave to dry.

2 Remove the template from the back of the glass. Paint over the leaves with the light green enamel paint, and leave to dry.

3 Paint a line of deep green paint along the lower edge of each of the light green leaves.

4 Paint the flowers with the red paint and then carefully blend in a little white towards the tips.

5 Paint over the stalk lines, half with raw sienna and half with yellow. Leave to dry.

Working
with Glass

Glass is a versatile medium to work with and can be used to create all sorts of accessories and decorations from trinket boxes to outdoor lanterns. Using glass that you have painted, or ready-coloured glass panels, learn to cut it safely and accurately into intricate shapes. With pieces cut to size, learn to solder them together to form three-dimensional functional pieces, or learn to add lead came to replicate stained glass windows.

Glorious Glassware

There is a lot more to glass than a flat surface on which to paint patterns or pictures. As a material, it provides a wonderfully versatile basis for a variety of applications. Stained glass is the most obvious one, where pieces of coloured glass are fixed together with strips of lead to create glorious patterns and pictures. Stained glass need not be as ambitious as that seen in church and cathedral windows – simple shaped dec-

orations can be made to hang in a window, so the sunlight can sparkle through the glass, or on a Christmas tree where the tree lights can brighten the rich colours of the decoration. Jewel-bright glass nuggets can be used together with coloured glass pieces for a three-dimensional effect.

In addition to creating pictures and decorations for the window, coloured

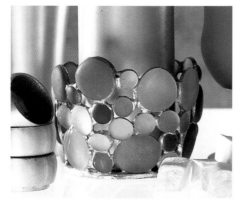

glass can be used to make vases, pots, trinket boxes and simple lanterns. The more ambitious could even create entire leaded door panels. Although not for the novice, this type of glasswork is only a step on from creating pictures, hangings and plaques.

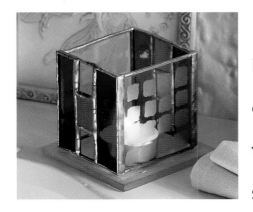

The traditional method of making stained glass involves cutting and soldering the individual pieces of glass together using copper foil and lead, but there is a far simpler and quicker way of creating a similar effect using self-adhesive lead strips. These are simply attached to the top of the glass to create the outlines of the design, and there is no cutting or soldering involved.

Glass cutting is not just for the professionals, and even the most experienced glass worker has to start somewhere. To minimize risks of cutting yourself from broken glass, always follow safety procedures, wear the correct clothing and protect your

eyes with goggles – no matter how small the task in hand. Similarly soldering can appear to be quite a daunting task. Learning to use equipment and materials properly will remove the fear. As with most things, you will find that the more often you practise, the more proficient you will become, and the more you will enjoy the versatility of this skilled craft.

A variety of materials is needed for working with glass, which include glass paints, solder and flux, all of which are readily available from specialist glass shops.

Materials

lengths. The central bar or heart keeps two pieces of glass apart when put together. The flat strips at the top and bottom of the heart – the leaf – will stop the glass from falling out. Always wear rubber (latex) gloves or barrier cream when using lead.

Self-adhesive lead
This stick-on lead strip can be used to reproduce real lead came. Ensure a good seal by rubbing the lead with a boning peg, or the back of a teaspoon. Do not smoke or handle food while using lead, and keep it away from children. Wash your hands after use.

Solder
Made up of equal parts of tin and lead.

Tinned copper wire
This can be soldered easily. You can also tin wire with a soldering iron.

Ultraviolet glue
This glue hardens in daylight. It will not harden behind red glass, which blocks UV rays.

You will need the following items: acetate, carbon paper, clear varnish, contour paste, glass nuggets, glass paints, masking tape, paper towels, cotton buds (swabs), reusable putty adhesive, silver jewellery wire, white spirit (paint thinner), stained glass.

Copper foil and wire
A self-adhesive, heat-resistant tape, copper foil comes in various widths. Use it to bind glass edges prior to soldering. Copper wire is malleable and ideal for hooks and decoration. It is compatible with tin solder.

Epoxy glue
This strong glue hardens in minutes.

Float glass
Glaziers sell this clear polished glass.

Flux
This is brushed on to copper foil to clean it and lower the melting point of the solder so it flows more easily.

Horseshoe nails
Use to hold glass pieces in place as you work. Easy to remove, they reduce the risk of damage to glass and lead.

Lead came
Use lead came for creating stained glass windows. Available in 2m/2¼yd

For decorative glasswork, you will need a range of tools to equip you for the basic skills of glass cutting and soldering. The most important of these are described or listed below.

Equipment

Lead knife
A lead knife has a curved blade to help when cutting lead came.

Lead vice
A lead vice is useful for stretching pieces of lead came before cutting.

Letherkin tool
This is used to open up the leaf of the lead came after you have cut it.

Protective goggles
These are vital for eye protection when cutting glass.

Scythe stone
This removes the sharp edges from cut glass. Use on every piece.

Soldering iron
Use a 75-watt soldering iron. You will need a stand for the hot iron.

Tallow stick
Tallow is the traditional alternative to liquid soldering flux.

You will also find the following items useful: cotton rags, craft knife, jewellery pliers, nail polish remover, paintbrushes, pencils and pens, pliers, rubber (latex) gloves, ruler, scissors, self-healing cutting mat, sponges, thick straightedge, wire cutters, wire (steel) brush, wire (steel) wool.

Boning peg
Use to smooth down the adhesive lead to ensure good contact with the glass.

Cutting oil
This oil lubricates the cutting wheel of a glass cutter and helps to prevent small particles of glass from binding to the wheel.

Fid
A fid is used for pressing down copper foil and self-adhesive lead.

Flux brush
These inexpensive brushes are used to paint flux on copper foil.

Glass cutter
Run the wheel of a glass cutter over the glass to be cut, to create a score mark. The glass will break on the line when stressed.

Grozing pliers
These are used to take off any sharp shards of glass.

Before you begin to tackle any of the projects in this chapter, look through this section, which acts as an introduction to the basic skills you will need for working with glass with assurance.

Techniques

Cutting glass Measure accurately the area of glass you want to cut. There is no margin for error and mistakes cannot be rectified.

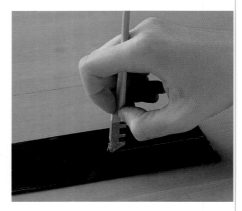

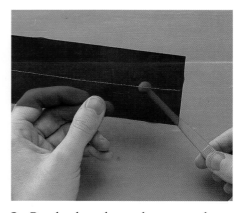

1 Hold the cutter so that your index finger is on top, your thumb and second finger grip each side, and the grozing teeth face towards your elbow. When you cut correctly with the cutter at a right angle to the glass, this position will give you movement in your arm.

2 Always cut the glass from edge to edge, one cut at a time. So start at one edge of the glass, with your cutter at right angles. Make it one continuous cut from one edge to the other.

3 Break the glass where you have made the score mark. Hold the cutter upside down between your thumb and first finger. Hold it loosely so that you can swing it to hit the underside of the score mark with the ball on the end of the cutter. Tap along the score mark. The glass will break.

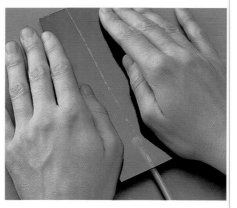

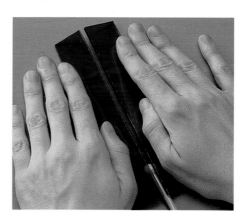

4 Alternatively, hold the glass at each side of the score mark. Apply firm pressure pulling down and away from the crack. Use this method for very straight lines.

5 You could try putting the cutter on the table with the glass on the cutter and score mark over the cutter. With the base of your thumbs put pressure on both sides of the score mark.

6 Break the glass along the score mark as shown. Smooth the edges and remove any sharp points with a scythe stone. Use a little water to lubricate the stone.

Foiling glass

Edging glass with copper foil allows you to solder pieces of glass together to create stained-glass effects. This technique is simple to do.

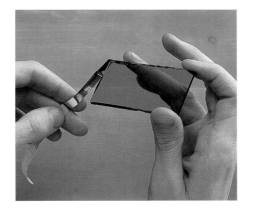

1 Hold the foil between your fingers, and use your thumb to peel back the protective backing paper as you work around the glass. Try not to touch the adhesive side of the tape – it will not stick if it is greasy or dusty.

2 Stick the foil to the edge of the piece of glass, working all the way around it, and overlapping the end of the foil by 1cm/½in.

3 Using two fingertips, press the foil down on to both sides of the glass, all the way around. Now use the fid to flatten the foil on to the glass to ensure it is stuck firmly all the way around.

Soldering glass

Soldering is the technique of joining pieces of metal together, in this case copper foil-edged glass. This is a technique that requires some practice to achieve a neat, professional finish.

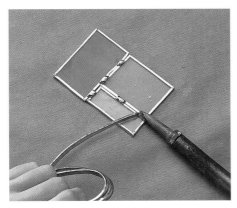

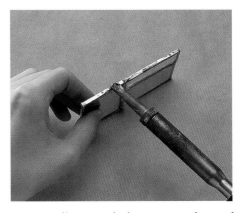

1 Using a flux brush, apply the flux to all the copper foil showing on the first side. Take the soldering iron so the tip of the iron side faces side to side and the thin side faces up and down. Hold the solder in the other hand with 10cm/4in uncoiled. Tack the pieces together by melting blobs of solder on to each joining edge. This holds the pieces while you solder them together.

2 Melt the solder, and allow it to run along the copper. Do not let it go too flat, but make sure you are always working with a small drop of solder. This makes it look neater and, even more importantly, is stronger. Turn the piece over and flux and solder the edges on the other side.

3 Tin all around the outer edges of the glass by firstly fluxing, and then running the soldering iron along the edges. There is usually enough solder from joining the inner edges to spread around the outside.

Using self-adhesive lead

Using self-adhesive lead is quick and easy. The skill is in the preparation: always ensure that the surface of the glass is scrupulously clean.

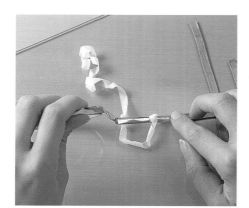

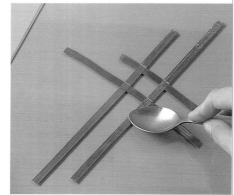

1 Clean the glass. Peel off the backing from the lead and press one end of it down gently with your fingers. Use one hand to hold the end while you bend the lead to fit the design. Always wash your hands after handling lead.

2 Trim the end with scissors. It is important that the lead strip is firmly stuck to the glass so that paint will not leak underneath it. After applying the strip, burnish it using a boning peg or the back of an old teaspoon.

Using lead came

This technique requires skill, but it is within everyone's reach. As special tools are needed for this technique, it can be expensive.

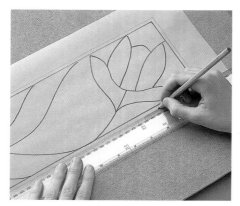

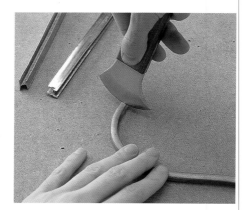

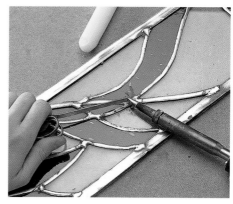

1 Draw the outline of each piece of glass that makes up the design. This outline represents the central point of the lead. Cut each piece of glass on the inside of the outline. To stretch the lead came to remove any kinks and make it easier to shape and cut, secure a spring-loaded vice to your bench and place one end of the came in it. Pull the other end with flat-nosed pliers. Do not break the lead.

2 Using a lead knife, bend the came to the shape of the edge of the glass. Using the knife blade, mark across the leaf where it will be cut (leave it a little short to accommodate the leaf of the piece crossing it). Place the came leaf on a flat surface. Position the knife and push down in a gentle but firm rocking motion until you are right through the came. Cut directly down and not at an angle.

3 Soldering wire for leaded panels contains lead, so wear barrier cream to protect your hands. Holding the soldering wire in your left hand, lower the tip of the soldering iron for a few seconds to melt the solder and join the separate pieces of lead came securely together.

This impressive panel is in the style of pictorial windows which were fashionable adornments for doors and porches in the 1930s. A gallant ship tossed on huge waves was a popular subject for this treatment.

Stained-glass Window

You will need

pane of glass to fit window

nail polish remover or glass cleaner

paper towels

scrap paper

felt-tipped pen

reusable putty adhesive

adhesive lead strip

tin snips or old scissors

boning peg or teaspoon

glass paints: red, yellow, dark blue, turquoise, white

medium and fine artist's paintbrushes

paint tray

1 Clean the glass to remove traces of grease. Draw a ship with hull and sails and waves on scrap paper to fit your panel and attach it to the underside of the glass using reusable putty adhesive.

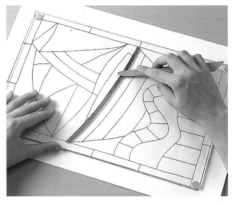

2 Peel the backing paper off a length of adhesive lead strip and place it over the line illustrating the hull of the boat. Trim the strip at the end with tin snips or old scissors, and smooth it down firmly using a boning peg or the back of a teaspoon, to ensure a good contact with the glass.

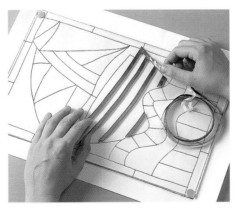

3 Repeat for the rest of the planks of the hull. Complete the outline of the boat, placing the strips over the ends of the previous ones. Trim the ends of the outline, and smooth down with either the boning peg or teaspoon.

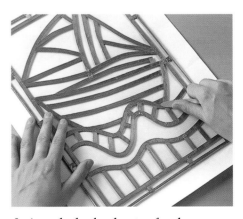

4 Attach the lead strips for the waves, positioning the long strips first. Ease the strips around the curves with your fingers. Complete the boat mast, sails and frame in the same way. Burnish all the lines with the boning peg or spoon, carefully smoothing the fullness on the inside of the curves. ▶

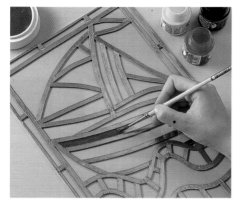

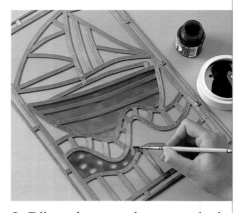

5 Mix burnt orange from the red and yellow paint and add a touch of dark blue. Paint the top plank of the hull with orange. For the next plank, mix a brighter orange. Add more of the yellow still to make light orange for the third plank, and paint the lowest plank yellow.

6 Fill in the central wave with the turquoise paint, leaving some small randomly spaced circles of clear glass.

7 Use dark blue to paint around the edge of the first panel in the lowest part of the sea. Mix the paint with white and add a pale blue strip down the middle of the panel while the dark blue is still wet. Draw the edges of the colours together for a marbled effect.

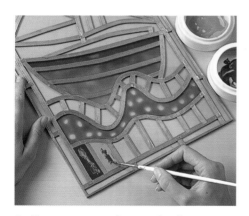

8 Repeat in each panel, alternating the colours. Above the wave, paint alternate panels dark or pale blue, leaving the remaining panels clear.

9 Mix the red with dark blue to make purple, and paint the cabin roof. Paint alternate panels of the sails yellow, then add a little blue paint to make a light green colour for the remaining parts of the sails.

10 Mix white with the light green and use to paint alternate panels of the frame. Paint the flag with the red paint. Mix turquoise with pale blue for the remaining panels of the frame. Leave the glass panel to dry completely.

Give your pictures a touch of grandeur with this richly coloured frame made from glass paints and stick-on lead in an abstract linear design. Choose colours to complement those in the picture you are framing.

Leaded Picture Frames

You will need
clean glass clip-frame
paper
pen and pencil
metal ruler
indelible black felt-tipped pen
3mm/⅛in self-adhesive lead
craft knife
self-healing cutting mat
boning peg
glass paints
paintbrush

1 Remove the clips and backing board from the clip-frame. Place the glass on a piece of paper and draw around it to create a template of the right dimensions.

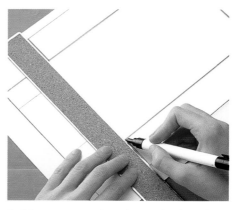

2 Using a pencil and metal ruler, draw a simple linear design on the template. Place the glass over the template and trace the design on to the glass using an indelible black felt-tipped pen.

3 Stretch the lead by pulling it gently. Cut four lengths to fit around the outside edge of the frame, using a sharp craft knife and a cutting mat. Remove the backing paper from the lead and stick the lead in place.

4 Measure the lead needed for the inner framework and cut with a craft knife by using a side-to-side rocking motion. Hold the knife blade at a 90-degree angle to the lead to ensure a straight cut. Work on a cutting mat. With the edges butted closely together, peel away the backing paper from the lead strips and press gently into place with your fingertips.

5 Once the lead is in the correct position, press firmly along its length using a boning peg to seal it to the glass.

6 With the pointed end of the boning peg, press around the outer edges of each strip of lead. This will tidy the edges and prevent the glass paints from seeping underneath the strips.

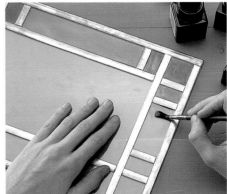

7 Colour in the design using glass paints. Leave to dry. Replace the backing board, add a picture of your choice and clip the frame into place.

This plain vase has been given a stained-glass effect with the use of vivid paints and patterns of stick-on lead. Filling the vase with water will ensure that the horizontal lines of the border will be accurate.

Banded Vase

You will need
square vase
water-based felt-tipped pen
ruler
black contour paste
sponge scourer
scissors
glass paints: yellow, orange, red
and violet
colourless medium
spatula
craft knife
self-healing cutting mat
3mm/¹⁄₈in self-adhesive lead
fid

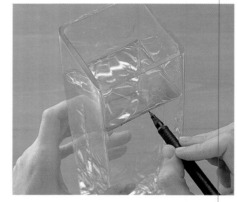

1 Gauge by eye the position of the borders. Using a water-based felt-tipped pen, draw the position of the lower border. Pour water into the vase up to this point. Stand the vase on a level surface and draw around the vase at the water level.

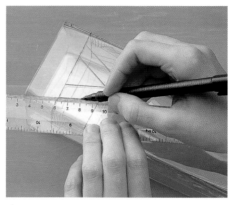

2 Mark the position of the top border. Top up the water to this level and draw the second line around the vase. Mark the simple pattern on to the surface of the vase with the felt-tipped pen and a ruler.

3 Go over the lines with the black contour paste and leave it to dry. Cut a sponge scourer into pieces to match the shapes of the design.

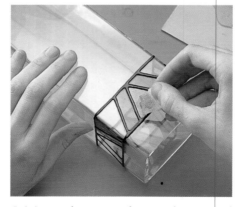

4 Mix each paint colour with an equal amount of colourless medium and sponge the paint over the vase using a different piece of sponge for each colour. Leave to dry for 24 hours.

5 Using a craft knife, score around the edge of each area of colour. Use the tip of the craft knife to lift up the contour paste and carefully peel it off the vase.

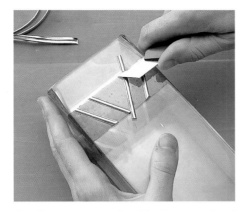

6 Cut pieces of self-adhesive lead slightly oversize for all of the shorter lines. Peel off the backing paper and press them in place. Trim the ends of each piece of lead at an angle with a craft knife.

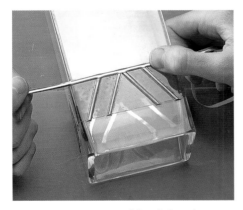

7 Cut two strips of lead for the two border lines and press them into place.

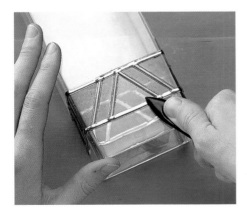

8 Rub over all the lead lines with a fid to press them firmly in place.

This piece of decorated glass creates beautiful shimmering patterns as it catches the light. The design is traced directly on to the glass with contour paste then coloured with glass paints.

Heart Light Catcher

You will need

paper

2mm/¹⁄₁₆in float glass

glass cutter

cutting oil

thick straightedge

self-adhesive copper foil tape

fid

1mm/¹⁄₂₅in tinned copper wire

wire cutters

round-nosed pliers

straight-nosed pliers

flux and flux brush

solder and soldering iron

black contour paste

glass paints: yellow, green, pink, blue and red

fine artist's paintbrush

paint palette

toothpick

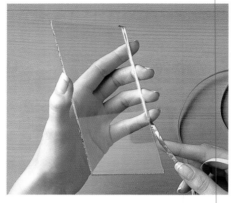

1 Enlarge the template from the back of the book and cut a piece of float glass to fit the design. Wash the glass and edge it with self-adhesive copper foil tape. Press down with a fid.

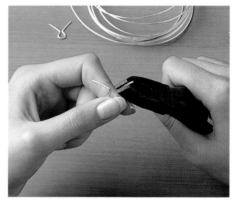

2 Bend the wire into two small circular hanging loops using round-nosed pliers. Grip the wire in the middle and bend the ends down to form an upside-down "U". With straight-nosed pliers, grip each arm of the "U" and bend up to form a 90-degree angle. Bend the arms downwards with round-nosed pliers.

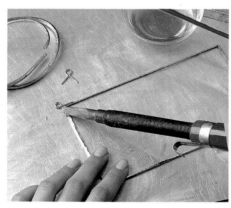

3 Brush the copper-foiled edge with flux, and then tin (see Window Hanging, step 4). Solder the hanging hoops in place. Wash the glass.

4 Lay the template on a work surface and place the light catcher over it. Trace the design on to the glass with black contour paste. Leave to dry.

5 Paint the glass, following the final photograph for the colours. Use the toothpick to decorate the design with scratchwork.

The simple materials of muslin (cheesecloth) fabric, coloured glass and silver wire complement each other perfectly to create this fresh and pleasingly uncluttered decoration.

Glass Nugget Window Hanging

You will need

pencil

paper

0.5m/¾yd white muslin (cheesecloth)

sharp scissors

white sewing thread

sewing needle

copyright-free pictures of shells

acetate

epoxy glue

4 large glass nuggets

fine silver jewellery wire

jewellery pliers

thick copper wire

1 Sketch your design to scale on a piece of paper. Draw the shape of the background on to the white muslin (cheesecloth) leaving extra to turn and edge the sides. Cut out the shape.

2 Using the white sewing thread, sew a single hem along each long side edge, then at the top and bottom.

3 Photocopy shell pictures on to acetate, so that they are slightly smaller than the glass nuggets. Cut out the images using sharp scissors.

4 Glue the acetate shapes on to the muslin, spacing them equally down the muslin. Then glue the glass nuggets over the images. Make sure they do not stick to your worktop as the glue may seep through.

5 Cut pieces of silver wire long enough to fit across each glass nugget, leaving a little extra at each side. Curl each end into a spiral shape using the jewellery pliers.

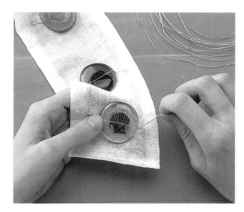

6 Sew the pieces of wire securely to the muslin rectangle at each side of the glass nuggets.

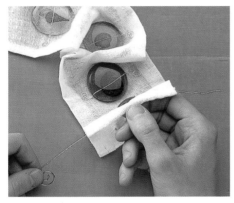

7 Take the copper wire, curl one end into a spiral using the small pliers, and slide the metal through the top hem of the muslin. Use another length of wire to do the same on the bottom. Curl the other end of both pieces of wire into matching spirals.

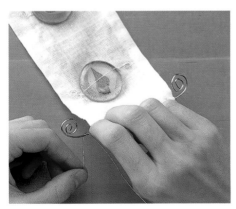

8 Take some silver wire and wind it round the copper wire at the top end, on both sides of the muslin, for the piece to hang in the window.

Pressed foliage and flowers are positioned on pieces of opaque blue glass and clear glass is placed on top. The wire that is wound round each pair of glass rectangles is both structural and decorative.

Flower and Foliage Wallhanging

You will need

6 pieces each of coloured glass and

matching-sized clear glass

tweezers

dried, pressed foliage

instant bonding adhesive

masking tape

1mm/¹⁄₂₅in copper wire

ruler

round-nosed pliers

straight-nosed pliers

1 Get your chosen coloured glass cut to size. Lay it on the work surface and, using tweezers, position pressed leaves on to the glass, fixing with a small dab of instant bonding adhesive.

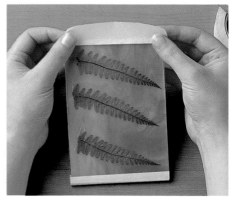

2 Place the clear glass over the leaves and apply strips of masking tape over the short edges to hold the two pieces of glass together temporarily.

3 Cut a piece of 1mm/¹⁄₃₂in copper wire 32cm/12½in long. Gripping the middle with round-nosed pliers, bend the ends down and twist them together with straight-nosed pliers.

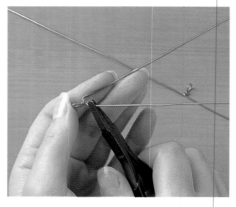

4 Use the pliers to bend out two ends of the wire horizontally, then make an "elbow" on both sides to fit over the edges of the glass.

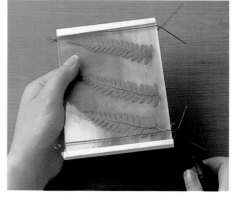

5 Position the wire around the glass and, using your fingers, bend the two ends over the edge. Use straight-nosed pliers to twist and close.

6 With round-nosed pliers, bend the two ends up into loops, forming a strong split ring. Trim off the excess wire to 1.5cm/⅝in.

7 Cut a piece of wire 18cm/7in long and repeat steps **3** to **6**. Link the second panel by linking the top loop and split ring. Remove the masking tape. Repeat for all the panels.

8 Carefully arrange the completed wallhanging face downwards, and make sure all of the wires are aligned. Press strips of masking tape over the wire on the back to hold it in place.

This vase evokes the work of the designer Charles Rennie Mackintosh. Self-adhesive lead is used to create the effect of leaded glasswork and is simply pressed on to the glass surface for a decorative effect.

Cherry Blossom Vase

You will need

paper

pencil

vase

reusable putty adhesive

self-adhesive lead, 3mm/⅛in and 4mm/³⁄₁₆in wide

scissors or craft knife

fid or wooden peg

glass paints: white and pink

matt varnish

paint-mixing palette

fine artist's paintbrush

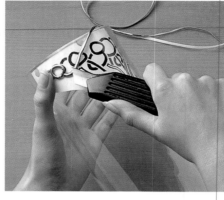

1 Enlarge the template from the back of the book to fit your vase. Stick it to the inside of the vase with reusable putty adhesive. Using the template as a guide, bend and stick the pieces of 3mm/⅛in-wide self-adhesive lead down over all of the bold lines on the template. Use scissors or a strong craft knife to trim the ends.

2 For the stem lines, cut two strips of 3mm/⅛in-wide self-adhesive lead the same length as your vase, and a further two 4mm/³⁄₁₆in-wide lead strips. Press the end of each into place to join the stems on the upper design and then run them down the length of the vase.

3 Splay the ends slightly at the base, and trim them so that they all end at the same point.

4 Cut a piece of 4mm/³⁄₁₆in-wide lead long enough to go around the vase with a little spare. Press it around the vase, just overlapping the edges of the stem lines. To smooth the joins, rub over with a fid or wooden peg.

5 Mix a little white paint with matt varnish. Do the same with a little pink paint. Apply the white paint sparingly to fill the blossom shapes, adding just a touch of pink to each area.

The etched glass panels on this old door have been painted with coloured glass paints and finished with stick-on lead strips. The finished effect has a lighter look than genuine stained glass.

Leaded Door Panels

You will need

door with two sandblasted
glass panels
tape measure
paper
pencil
ruler
black felt-tipped pen
scissors
masking tape
indelible black felt-tipped pen
self-adhesive lead, 1cm/⅜in wide
craft knife
self-healing cutting mat
boning peg
glass paints: turquoise, green, yellow
and light green
turpentine
fine artist's paintbrushes

1 Measure the glass panels with a tape measure. With a pencil, draw them to scale on a piece of paper. Using a ruler, draw your design within the panel area, including 1cm/⅜in wide dividing lines to allow for the leading. Trace over the design in felt-tipped pen, cross-hatching the lead lines.

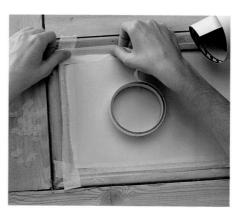

2 Cut out this paper pattern carefully with scissors and then stick it to the reverse of one of the glass panels by applying lengths of masking tape around the edges.

3 Trace the design from the pattern on to the sandblasted side of the glass with an indelible black felt-tipped pen. When the tracing is complete, remove the paper pattern.

4 Stretch the lead by gently pulling it. Cut four lengths to fit around the edge of the glass panel, using a sharp craft knife. Remove the backing paper and stick the lead in place.

5 Measure the lead needed for the inner framework and cut with a craft knife using a side-to-side rocking motion. Keep the blade at a 90-degree angle to the lead to ensure a straight cut. Cut and stick longer lengths of lead first, then work the smaller pieces.

6 With the edges butted closely together, remove the backing paper from the lead and press into place with your fingertips. Then press firmly along the length of the lead with a boning peg to seal it to the glass. Press around the outer edges of the lead lines with the pointed end of the boning peg in order to create a neat, watertight finish.

7 Dilute the glass paints with 30 per cent turpentine to create a subtle, watercolour feel to the paint. Use a small paintbrush to colour in the small areas between the leading. Clean the brushes with turpentine between the different colours.

8 Once the intricate areas are coloured in, paint the remainder of the design, leaving the centre of the glass panel unpainted. Alternatively, you could paint the whole area if you prefer. Repeat for the other panel.

The fresh white and green opal glass of this planter neatly hides the flowerpot inside, while the contrasting colours of the opal glass will complement the colour of the foliage.

Opal Glass Planter

You will need
tracing paper
black pen and paper
white and green opal glass
glass cutter
straightedge
round-nosed pliers
carbon paper
ballpoint pen
scythe stone
5mm/¼in-wide copper foil
fid
solder and soldering iron
flux
flux brush
washing-up liquid (dishwashing detergent)

1 Trace the template from the back of the book, enlarging to the size required. Place the white glass over the template and score five identical pieces for the sides with a glass cutter, using a straightedge to ensure straight lines. Use a pair of round-nosed pliers to break the glass along the scorelines. Cut strips of green opal glass for the bottom of each panel.

2 Place carbon paper over the green glass, then put the template on top. Transfer the shape for the top sections with a pen. Score the straight lines using a straightedge as a guide. Score the curved edges and break them by tapping under the glass with the ball on the end of the glass cutter. Transfer and cut out the base design. Remove sharp edges with a scythe stone.

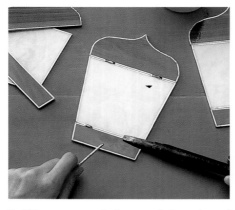

3 Wrap copper foil around the edge of each piece and use a fid to press the foil into place. Allow the soldering iron to heat up. Brush on flux and tack-solder together the three sections that make up each side panel.

4 Lightly tack-solder one of the side panels to the base, using a minimum of solder. Position the next panel and repeat. Tack the two panels together. Continue until all the pieces are in place on the base.

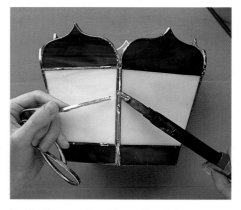

5 Reflux and solder all of the joints. Wash the planter thoroughly before use, with hot water and washing-up liquid (dishwashing detergent).

In this unusual project, different-sized glass nuggets are gradually built up one on top of another to create a colourful wall around the mirrored base of the bottle holder. Choose a whole rainbow of beautiful colours.

Glass Nugget Bottle Holder

You will need

self-healing cutting mat

pair of compasses (compass)

indelible black felt-tipped pen

mirror glass

bottle

glass cutter

square-nosed pliers

copper foil, 12mm/½in and

4mm/³⁄₁₆in wide

fid

solder

soldering iron

flux

flux brush

glass nuggets

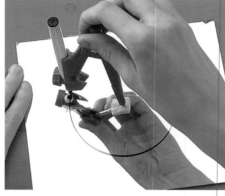

1 On a cutting mat draw a circle on mirror glass 2.5–4cm/1–1½in larger than the base of the bottle.

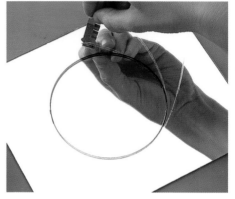

2 Score around the circle with a glass cutter. Draw lines from the edge of the circle to the edge of the mirror.

3 Tap on the reverse of the mirror with the ball of the glass cutter.

4 Loosen and then break off the excess mirror with square-nosed pliers.

5 Wrap the 12mm/½in copper foil around the edge of the glass circle.

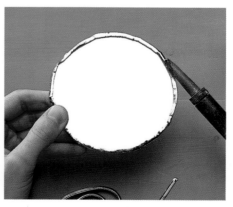

6 Press down with a fid and solder using flux and the soldering iron.

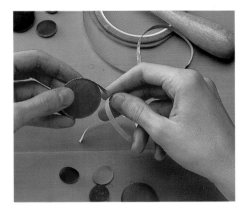

7 Select some of the coloured glass nuggets and wrap each one with the 4mm/³⁄₁₆in copper foil.

8 Solder the nuggets and start to build up an edge around the glass circle.

9 When the border is the required height, tidy up the inside and outside with the soldering iron to smooth out any drips of solder.

Slip this glass lantern over a night-light to create a colourful glow in the evenings. The lantern is made with two plain and two panelled sections of coloured glass.

Indoor Glass Lantern

You will need
tracing paper
pencil
ruler and pen (optional)
glass cutter
sheets of clear glass
sheets of stained glass: red, orange and yellow
etching paste
medium artist's paintbrush
clean cotton rag
5mm/¼in copper foil
fid
flux and flux brush
solder and soldering iron
small box or block of wood
night-light
tile

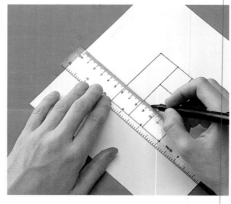

1 Trace the templates for the indoor lantern from the back of the book. Enlarge to the size required using a ruler and pen or a photocopier.

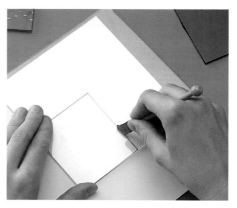

2 Take a glass cutter and, using your templates as a guide, cut out two clear glass sides and the pieces of coloured glass for the other two sides. You will have four red pieces, three orange and three yellow.

3 Using the template as a guide, take each side and paint etching paste on in squares as shown. Leave the paste for 3 minutes.

4 Take the acid-etched glass to your sink and allow cold water to run freely over the glass to take the paste off. Rinse thoroughly and then dry with a clean cotton rag.

5 Wrap copper foil around the edges of all of the pieces of coloured and clear/etched glass. Using a fid, flatten all the copper foil to smooth around the edges.

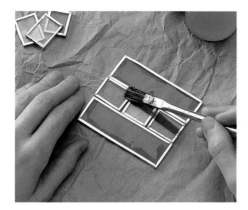

6 Place the pieces next to each other as you wish to solder them, panel by panel. Flux all the copper using a flux brush.

7 Tack each side together by melting a spot of solder on each joining edge. This keeps the pieces in place, and makes soldering easier.

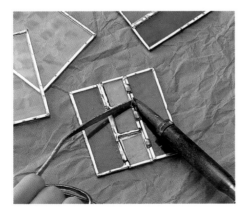

8 Solder each side together, and then solder around the edges to complete the four panels.

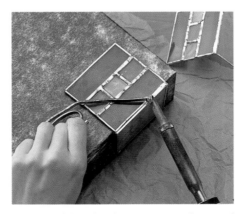

9 To solder the lantern together and make it three-dimensional you will need to balance the sides at a right angle on a small box or a block of wood. Flux and solder two corners so they can stand upright.

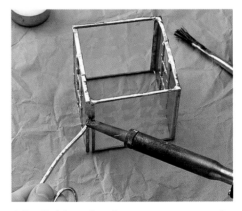

10 Solder the last two corners by fluxing and then soldering from top to bottom. Clean the glass with a clean cotton rag. Stand the night-light on a tile and place the lantern over it.

This plaque is made from pieces of stained glass and glass nuggets. Nuggets come in a wide range of colours and can add bright spots of colour among the crazy patchwork of glass.

Door Number Plaque

You will need

circle cutter

cutting oil

30cm/12in square of 3mm/⅛in

clear glass

piece of carpet or blanket

glass cutter

tracing paper

pencil

paper

indelible black felt-tipped pen

pieces of stained glass

scythe stone

glass nuggets

ultraviolet glue

lead came

lead knife

bradawl or drill

2mm/¹⁄₁₆in copper wire

round-nosed pliers

flux and flux brush

solder

soldering iron

black acrylic paint

tiling grout

grout spreader

clean cotton rag

Tip
Glass glue sets when it is exposed to ultraviolet light or sunlight.

1 Set a circle cutter to cut a 20cm/8in diameter circle. Dip the cutter in oil, centre it in the glass square and score the circle in one sweep. Turn the glass over and place it on a piece of carpet or blanket on a work surface. Press down with both thumbs just inside the scoreline until the line begins to break. Repeat until the scoreline is broken all the way around.

2 Use a glass cutter to score a line in from each corner of the glass square, stopping just before you reach the circle. With the ball of the glass cutter, tap behind each scored line until the glass cracks up to the circle. The side sections will fall away, releasing the circle.

3 Trace the templates from the back of the book, enlarging them to the size required. Draw around the circle of glass on to plain paper and write your own door number centrally using the template as a guide.

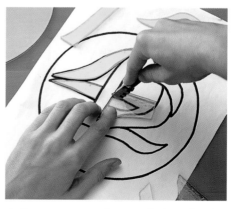

4 Score pieces of stained glass for the numerals. Break the glass by tapping behind the scoreline with the ball of the glass cutter. Remove any rough edges with a scythe stone. Centre the glass circle over the template.

5 Arrange the numerals on the glass circle and place glass nuggets around them. Cut pieces of glass in contrasting colours to fill the spaces. Working away from sunlight, apply ultraviolet glue to the back of each piece and press it into place. When all of the pieces are glued, check the position of each and slide them into place.

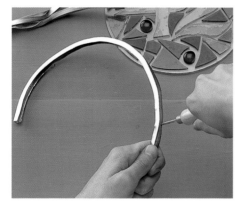

6 Use a lead knife to cut a length of lead came approximately 70cm/28in long. Use a bradawl or drill to make a small hole in the centre of the strip of came.

7 Cut a 10cm/4in length of copper wire. With a pair of round-nosed pliers, bend a hanging loop. Thread the ends through the hole in the came and bend them up to lock the loop in place. Wrap the came around the glass with the hanging loop at the top.

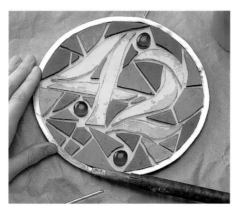

8 Trim off any excess lead came with the lead knife. Flux the joint and then lightly solder the ends together.

9 Mix some black paint with grout. Spread it over the surface, into the spaces between the glass. Remove any excess with a rag. Leave to dry, then polish with a clean cotton rag.

The type of paintwork used in this unusual window decoration is not very easy to control, and it is precisely this free-flowing quality that gives the style its appeal.

Window Hanging

You will need

paper and pencil

glass, 3mm/⅛in thick

glass cutter

cutting oil

scythe stone

5mm/¼in self-adhesive copper foil tape

fid

red glass nuggets

flux and flux brush

solder and soldering iron

1mm/¹⁄₂₅in tinned copper wire

round-nosed pliers

straight-nosed pliers

black contour paste

paint-mixing palette

glass paints: blue, turquoise, red, yellow, violet and white

clear varnish

fine artist's paintbrush

1 Enlarge the template at the back of the book to a size that is suitable for the window you wish to hang the pieces in. Lay a sheet of glass on the template and cut out five sections. (Have a glazier do this if you are not confident in cutting glass.)

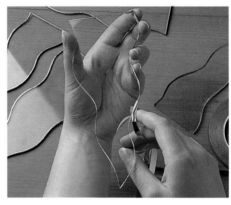

2 Wash all of the pieces to remove any traces of cutting oil. Remove any sharp edges with a scythe stone, then press self-adhesive copper foil tape over all of the edges. Press the foil down with a fid.

3 Using a scythe stone, lightly abrade the edge of each glass nugget. Wrap each nugget in copper foil tape.

4 Brush all of the copper-foiled edges with flux. Melt a bead of solder on to your soldering iron, and run the bead along the edge of each piece of glass to "tin" it with a thin coating of solder. Repeat as necessary until all of the edges are equally coated. Cut ten pieces of tinned copper wire 5cm/2in long for the hanging loops.

5 With round-nosed pliers, bend the ends down to form an upside-down "U". With straight-nosed pliers, grip each arm of the "U" and bend it up to form a 90-degree angle. Grip with round-nosed pliers while you bend the two arms downwards. Touch-solder the loops on the top of the glass pieces. Wash the pieces.

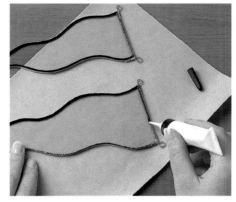

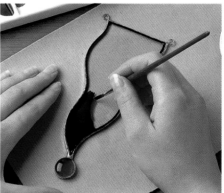

6 Apply flux to the end of one of the sections and one of the nuggets. Melt a bead of solder on to the iron and then solder the nugget in place. Melt on some more solder to ensure the nugget is secure.

7 Apply a line of black contour paste around the edge of each of the glass pieces in order to contain the glass paint solution.

8 In a mixing palette, prepare the colours you wish to use. Mix each with equal parts of clear varnish and opaque white paint. Apply the colours thickly and freely, allowing them to blend into each other. Leave to dry for at least 24 hours.

These square and triangular stained-glass pendants are decorated with motifs cut from acetate. Hang them in a line on a gauzy fabric curtain to allow the sunlight and colours to really shine through.

Curtain Decorations

You will need

copyright-free pictures of shells

acetate

small, sharp scissors

pencil

paper

tracing paper

pieces of stained glass

glass cutter

4mm/³⁄₁₆in copper foil

fid

flux and flux brush

solder and soldering iron

epoxy glue

copper wire

small pliers

hooks and eyes

white sewing thread

sewing needle

white muslin (cheesecloth) curtain

curtain pole

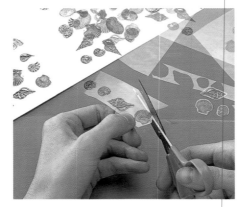

1 Photocopy pictures of shells on to acetate and cut them out with small, sharp scissors.

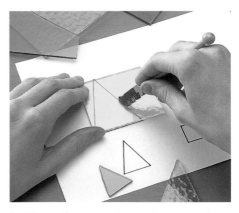

2 Trace the triangles and squares from the back of the book. Cut out glass shapes, using the templates as a guide.

3 Wrap copper foil around the edges of the larger pieces of glass.

4 Use a fid to flatten the edges of the copper foil around the pieces of glass.

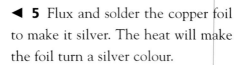

◀ **5** Flux and solder the copper foil to make it silver. The heat will make the foil turn a silver colour.

▶ **6** Take a soldered piece of glass and a smaller piece of the same shape. Glue the pieces together, trapping the photocopy between the glass.

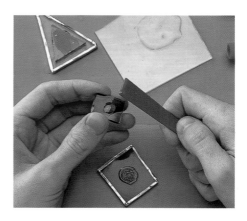

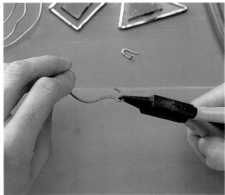

7 Using a pair of small pliers, bend the copper wire into small hooks. Make a separate hook for each decoration you have made.

8 Solder the hook to the copper foil around the edges of the decorations, remembering to flux the wire and the soldered edges.

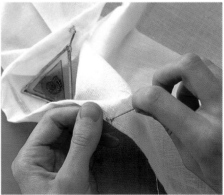

9 Sew the eyes from several hooks and eyes to the top of the curtain and hook on the curtain decorations. Fold the curtain over a pole so the decorations are hanging in the top third of the window, as shown.

Opal glass is available from stained-glass specialists and has an extra special lustre. As this project involves cutting and soldering lots of small pieces, it is intended for the more experienced glassworker.

Trinket Box

You will need

carbon paper

paper

pencil

clear 2mm/¹⁄₁₆in picture glass

blue opal glass

mirrored blue stained glass

cutting square or straightedge

glass cutter

cutting oil

copper foil, 4mm/³⁄₁₆in and 5mm/¹⁄₄in

fid

flux

flux brush

soldering iron

solder

tinned copper wire

wire cutters

indelible black felt-tipped pen

scythe stone

round-nosed pliers

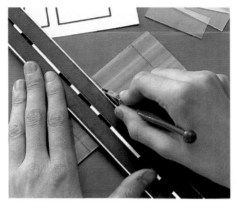

1 Enlarge the template from the back of the book to the size required. Transfer the shapes to the glass using carbon paper. Transfer the side pieces of the box on to clear glass and blue opal glass, and the octagonal base outline on to the mirrored blue glass. Score and break the glass using a thick straightedge or a cutting square.

2 Wrap the edges of the blue opal side pieces in 5mm/¹⁄₄in-wide copper foil and the edges of the thinner clear picture glass in the 4mm/³⁄₁₆in-wide copper foil. Press the foil down firmly using a fid.

3 Apply lines of 4mm/³⁄₁₆in-wide copper foil along the edges of the top surface of the mirror base to ensure that the sides bond firmly to the base. Wrap the sides in 5mm/¹⁄₄in-wide copper foil. Press down firmly with a fid.

4 Brush all of the copper-wrapped pieces with safety flux and lightly tack-solder the pieces into place, adjusting them slightly if necessary.

▶

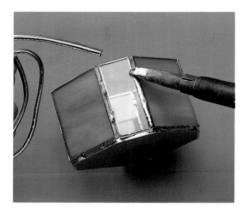

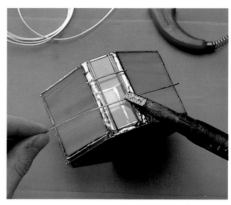

5 Reflux and solder all the copper surfaces. To give the edges a neat finish, run a bead of solder to fill the point where the side sections meet. Wash the box thoroughly to remove any traces of flux.

6 With the box balanced on one side, hold the end of a piece of wire just overlapping one of the clear sections. Brush with flux and touch the tip of the iron to the wire to solder it. Trim off the other end with wire cutters and repeat, using two vertical wires for each clear glass panel.

7 Solder two horizontal pieces of wire to each pair of verticals. Solder them on oversize, then trim them to length when they are soldered in place. Wash thoroughly to remove any traces of flux. Repeat steps 6 and 7 for each clear glass pane.

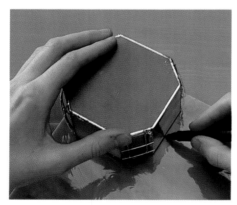

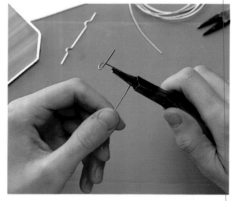

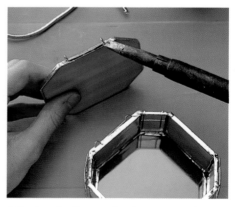

8 Choose some glass for the lid and place it with the side you want to be uppermost facing down. Place the box upside down over the glass and trace around the box with an indelible black felt-tipped pen. Score and break the glass just inside the lines. Remove any extra sharp edges with a scythe stone lubricated with a little water, then wrap the edges of the lid in 5mm/¼in-wide foil. Apply flux and plate the foil with solder.

9 Cut a piece of wire measuring about 10cm/4in long. Bend two kinks in the wire with a pair of round-nosed pliers, using the picture as a guide. Cut another 10cm/4in length of wire and bend two right angles in it to coincide with the kinks in the first wire. Bend the two ends into loops and trim off the excess wire with the wire cutters.

10 Apply flux to both pieces of wire. Solder the kinked length of wire to one side of the box and the looped piece to the lid. Wash both the box and the lid thoroughly to remove any traces of flux. Slot the lid hinge section into the body section to complete the trinket box.

This stained-glass project uses many glass pieces that are cut to shape to create an abstract design, ideal for the panel of a bathroom cabinet. It is an ambitious project.

Bathroom Cabinet Door Panel

You will need

tracing paper

pencil

ruler

felt-tipped pen

sheets of coloured glass

glass cutter

grozing pliers

masking tape

wooden board

three battens

hammer and horseshoe nails

lead knife

15mm/⅝in lead came

letherkin tool

barrier cream

wire (steel) brush

tallow

clean cotton rags

solder wire and soldering iron

rubber (latex) gloves (optional)

black lead lighting putty

whiting powder

hard scrubbing brush

fire grate blackener

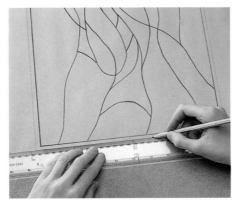

1 Trace the template from the back of the book, enlarging to the size required. The outer line represents the outer edge of the lead came. Go over the inner lines in felt-tipped pen. These thick lines will represent the centre of the pieces of lead came that join the glass together.

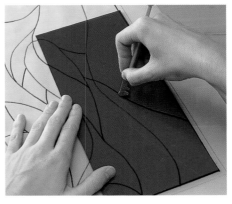

2 To cut out the coloured glass for the panel, lay a sheet of glass over the design and, starting from one corner, score along a line using a glass cutter. Carefully score along the other lines of the piece.

3 Use the ball end of the glass cutter to gently tap the reverse of the glass below the line you have scored. Tap until the two pieces fall apart. Use grozing pliers to nip off any small pieces of glass.

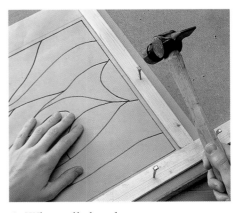

4 When all the glass is cut, tape your drawing to a wooden board. Nail one batten to each side edge and another to the bottom edge, along the outer pencil line of the rectangle.

▶

5 Using a lead knife, mark and cut a piece of lead came to fit along the side of the panel. Repeat for the bottom edge. Using a letherkin tool, open up the leaves of the lead to make it easier to insert the glass. Wear barrier cream to protect your hands from the toxic lead.

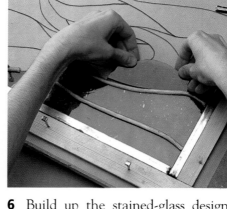

6 Build up the stained-glass design one piece at a time, cutting the lead came and inserting the glass carefully between the leaves of lead. Hammer horseshoe nails into the wooden board, as shown, to tack and hold the lead in place as you work.

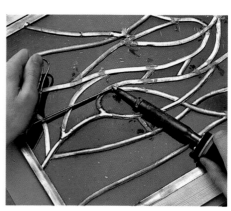

7 When the design is finished, clean the lead joints with a wire (steel) brush. Rub tallow on to each joint. Place solder wire over the joint then melt into place with the soldering iron. When the front is finished, turn the panel over and repeat the process on the reverse.

8 Wearing barrier cream, use your thumbs to press black lead lighting putty firmly into the gaps between the lead came and the pieces of glass. Work around the border and all around the individual pieces.

9 Cover the glass panel liberally with whiting powder. This will absorb the excess oil in the putty and help it to dry more quickly. Leave to harden for 1–2 hours. Use a hard scrubbing brush to clean off the whiting and excess putty. Repeat steps 8 and 9 on the reverse of the panel.

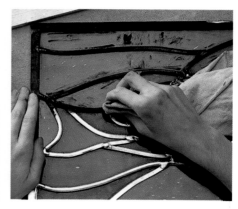

10 Wearing barrier cream, coat the lead with fire grate blackener using a clean cotton rag, then polish off the excess until you get a deep colour.

Glass Mosaic

Mosaic is a craft achievable by complete beginners. Essentially, it is painting-by-numbers but with pieces of glass, known as tesserae, instead of paint. The skill lies in combining colours together in a pleasing way, and in producing a representative pictorial image. To start with, draw simple stylized shapes freehand or mark out geometric patterns on a plywood base, then fill in the designs with coloured glass tesserae.

Mosaic Masterpieces

Creating a glass mosaic is very satisfying, particularly for those who enjoy finely detailed work. Made with pieces of vitreous glass, a mosaic has a striking, fragmented look and a lovely textural finish. Vitreous glass tesserae are manufactured glass squares that can easily be cut into different shapes with tile nippers to fit a design. When embarking on your first mosaic, choose a small-scale, simple design to work on an object such as a plant pot or house number plate.

Geometric shapes, stripes and swirls work well. Often, these simple designs can produce the most effective mosaics. Concentrate on combining different colours in the tesserae you choose. Lay the tesserae side-by-side and look at the effect of the different elements. When the combinations work, you can commit yourself to

sticking the tesserae to the base.

Mosaics can be flat and two-dimensional, such as plaques, panels and picture frames, or they can be three-dimensional, such as those decorating trinket boxes, lamp stands and plant pots. With two-

dimensional mosaic it is possible to see how the colours work together in an instant, unlike three-dimensional designs. Dark and light tesserae placed side-by-side produce a bold, striking effect while colours with similar tonal value produce a more subtle shading.

In a mosaic, grout can be as important as the tesserae. It holds the pieces together and unifies the design. Grout is available in powder form or ready mixed in white, beige, grey and black. It is possible to add acrylic paint or dye to the grout mix in a colour that is appropriate for your colour scheme to offset the mosaic. Determine what role the

grout should play, and therefore what colour it should be, when planning your design.

In this chapter, you will find plenty of ideas for making door plaques, mosaic lanterns, plant pots, boxes, bottles, tables, and even a stained-glass screen. Follow the projects step-by-step, or use them as a springboard for your own creative ideas for mosaics.

The main materials used in mosaic are the individual pieces, known as tesserae, which can be ceramic, glass, china or any solid material. The other important material to consider is the base, which should be rigid.

Materials

Grout

Specialist grouts are smoother than tile adhesive and are available in a variety of colours.

Shellac

Use this to seal finished mosaics, especially those for outside use.

Tesserae

Mosaic material is described as tesserae.

Ceramic tiles – These are available in a range of colours and textures, glazed or unglazed. Household tiles can be cut to size using a hammer, or tile nippers for precise shapes.

China – Old china makes unusual tesserae. It creates an uneven surface, so is suitable for decorative projects rather than flat, functional surfaces. Break up china using a hammer.

Marble – Marble can be bought pre-cut into small squares; to cut it with accuracy you need specialist tools.

Mirror glass – Shards of mirror add a reflective sparkle to a mosaic. Mirror can be cut with tile nippers or glass cutters, or broken with a hammer.

Smalti – This is opaque glass that has been cut into regular chunks. It has a softly reflective surface.

Vitreous glass tesserae – These are glass squares which are corrugated on the back to accommodate tile adhesive. They are hardwearing and thus perfect for outdoor projects.

Adhesives

There are several ways of attaching tesserae to a background. Cement-based tile adhesive is the most well known, and it can also be used to grout between the tesserae once the design is complete. For a wood base, use PVA (white) glue. For a glass base, use a silicone-based or a clear, all-purpose adhesive; to stick glass to metal, use epoxy resin. PVA is also used to prime a wooden base to make a suitable surface for the mosaic.

Admix

This is added to tile adhesive for extra adhesion.

Bases

Mosaic can be made on top of almost any rigid and pre-treated surface. One of the most popular bases is plywood.

Brown paper

This is used as backing for mosaics created by the semi-indirect method. Use the heaviest available.

Many of the tools needed to make mosaics are ordinary household equipment; the rest can be purchased in a good hardware store. A pair of tile nippers is the main piece of specialist equipment you will need.

Equipment

Clamps or bench vice
These are needed when cutting out the wooden base for projects.

Dilute hydrochloric acid
Use to clean cement-based grout from the finished mosaic if necessary. Always wear protective clothing, and work in a well-ventilated area.

Drill
A hand electric drill is needed for hanging projects on the wall.

Glass cutter
Use to cut or score glass tesserae.

Paint scraper
This is used to remove awkward pieces of dried tile adhesive or grout from the surface of a completed mosaic.

Protective face mask
You are strongly advised to wear a dust mask when you are mixing powdered grout, sanding the finished mosaic, and cleaning with hydrochloric acid.

Protective goggles
Wear safety goggles when you cut or smash tiles, and when working with hydrochloric acid.

Sacking (heavy cloth)
Use to wrap up tiles before breaking them with a hammer.

Sandpaper
Use coarse-grade sandpaper to prepare wood. To clean finished mosaics, use fine-grade sandpaper and wear a mask.

Saw
Use to cut wooden base material. Use a hacksaw for basic shapes, and a jigsaw for more complicated designs.

Spatula/Spreader/Squeegee
Used for spreading glue or other smooth adhesives, such as cellulose filler, on to your base material.

Tile nippers
These are invaluable for cutting shaped tiles, especially curves.

You will also find the following items useful: bradawl, chalk, craft knife, flexible knife, rubber (latex) gloves, hammer, felt-tipped pen, masking tape, mixing container, nailbrush, paintbrushes, pencil, plastic spray bottle, pliers, ruler, scissors, set square, sponge, tape measure.

Read the instructions below carefully before beginning a mosaic project and choose the methods most appropriate to the design that you are creating. Remember to wear protective clothing.

Techniques

Cutting tesserae

There are two methods of cutting tesserae, one using tile nippers and one using a hammer. Choose the method depending on the shape of tesserae you require.

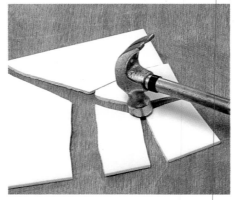

1 Using tile nippers and wearing goggles, hold a tesserae between the tips of the nippers, and squeeze the handles together. It should break along the line of impact. To cut a specific shape, nibble at the edges.

2 Use a hammer to break up larger pieces such as household tiles and china, where regular shapes are not required. Remember to wear protective goggles.

3 When working with a hammer it is also advisable to wrap each tile or plate in a piece of sacking or heavy cloth to prevent flying shards.

Cutting glass

This technique requires practice and is potentially more dangerous. Wear protective goggles and follow the instructions below.

1 Holding the glass cutter, rest your index finger along the top. Hold the cutter at a 90-degree angle to the glass.

2 Applying firm, even pressure, score a line across in a single movement, without a break. You can either push the cutter away from you or pull it towards you. Don't score over the same line; if you make a mistake, try again on another part of the glass.

3 Hold the scored piece of glass in one hand. With your working hand, place pliers along the scored line and grip them firmly.

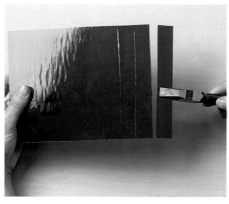

4 Angle the tip of the pliers up and pull down. The glass should break cleanly in two along the scored line.

Direct method

This is a popular technique, in which the tesserae are stuck, face up, on to the base and grouted into place. On a three-dimensional object or uneven surface this may be the only suitable method.

1 Cover the base with adhesive. Press the tesserae into it, cover with grout, leave to dry, then clean.

2 If you are following a design drawn on the base as a guide, apply a thin layer of tile adhesive on to the wrong side of each individual tessera and stick it into place.

3 If the tesserae are reflective, such as mirror glass or gold or silver smalti, try placing them at slightly different angles on a three-dimensional surface, to catch the light.

Semi-indirect method

With this method the tesserae are glued to the design off-site, but are then set into the tile adhesive in the final position.

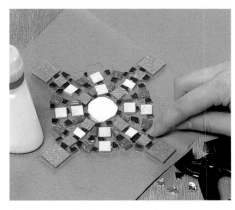

1 Draw a design on to brown paper. Adhere the tesserae right side down on to the paper using PVA (white) glue and a brush or palette knife.

2 Spread tile adhesive over the area designated for the mosaic. Press the mosaic into the adhesive, paper side up. Leave to dry for at least 24 hours.

3 Dampen the paper with a wet sponge and peel it off. The mosaic is now ready to be grouted and cleaned.

Indirect method

This technique originated as a way of making large mosaics off-site so that they could be transported ready-made. The design is divided into manageable sections which are fitted together on-site.

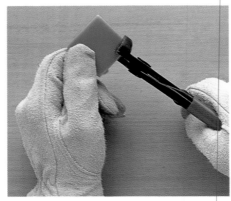

1 Make a wooden frame to the size required, securing the corners with 2.5cm/1in screws. Make a brown paper template of the inside of the frame. Draw a design on the design area of the paper, leaving a 5mm/¼in margin all around. Grease the inside of the frame with petroleum jelly.

2 Wearing protective goggles and gloves, cut the tesserae as required. Glue them right side down on the brown paper, using water-soluble adhesive and following the design. Leave to dry.

3 Place the wooden frame carefully over the mosaic, then sprinkle dry sand over the mosaic, using a soft brush to spread it into the crevices between the tesserae.

4 Wearing a face mask, on a surface that cannot be damaged, mix 3 parts sand with 1 part cement. Make a well in the centre, add water and mix it with a trowel until you have a firm consistency. Gradually add more water, if necessary, until the mortar is pliable but not runny.

5 Half-fill the frame with mortar, pressing it into the corners. Cut a square of chicken wire a little smaller than the frame. Place it on top of the mortar so that the wire does not touch the frame. Fill the rest of the frame with mortar, then smooth the surface. Cover with damp newspaper, then heavy plastic sheeting, and leave to dry thoroughly for 5–6 days.

6 Turn the frame over. Dampen the brown paper with a wet sponge and then carefully peel it off. Loosen the screws and remove the frame from the mosaic. The mosaic is now ready to be grouted and cleaned.

Grouting

Mosaics are grouted to give them extra strength and a smoother finish. Grout binds the tesserae together. Coloured grout is often used to unify the design; this can either be purchased as ready-made powder, or you can add dye or acrylic paint to plain grout.

1 When grouting three-dimensional objects or uneven surfaces, it is easiest to spread the grout with a flexible knife or spreader.

2 Rub the grout deep into the crevices in between the tesserae. Always wear rubber (latex) gloves when you are handling grout directly.

3 To grout large, flat mosaics, you can use powdered tile adhesive. Spoon it on to the surface, then spread it with a soft brush to fill all the crevices between the tesserae.

4 When you have completed the grouting process, spray the adhesive with water from a plastic spray bottle. You may need to repeat the process to achieve a smooth finish.

Cleaning

It is advisable to get rid of most of the excess grout while it is still wet. Most purpose-made grouts can be scrubbed from the surface using a stiff-bristled nailbrush and then polished off.

Cement mortars and cement-based adhesives need rougher treatment, and you will probably need to use sandpaper. A fast alternative is to dilute hydrochloric acid and then paint it on to the surface to dissolve the excess cement. The process should be done outside, as it gives off toxic fumes. When the excess cement has fizzed away, wash off the residue of acid from the mosaic with plenty of water. Remember to wear a face mask when sanding, and a face mask, goggles and gloves when using hydrochloric acid.

A mosaic door plaque adds a distinctive touch to your home and will withstand all weathers. Plan the design carefully so that you have space between the numbers and the border to fit neatly cut tesserae.

Door Number Plaque

1 Cut a piece of craft paper the same size as the tile. Mark the border and number in reverse on the shiny side of the paper. The border is one tessera wide. There should be room between the border and numbers to insert a quarter-tessera neatly.

2 Dilute the PVA (white) glue to a 50/50 solution with water. Glue the flat sides of the turquoise tesserae on to the border of the craft paper, with a single black tessera at each corner of the plaque.

3 Cut some black tesserae with the tile nippers to make rectangles. Glue the black rectangles flat-side down over the paper numbers.

4 Cut the yellow tesserae into quarter-squares. Lay them around the straight edges of the numbers, using the tile nippers to cut to size as necessary. Glue them flat-side down as before. Place quarter-square yellow tesserae all around the curved edges of the numbers, cutting as necessary.

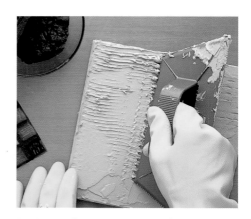

5 Mix the grout according to the manufacturer's instructions. Grout the mosaic with the spreader, removing the excess with a damp sponge. Leave to dry. Spread a layer of tile adhesive over the floor tile and key (scuff) with the notched edge of the spreader.

6 Place the grouted mosaic paper-side down on a flat surface. Place the floor tile on top, matching corners and edges. Press the tile down, wipe away excess adhesive and leave to dry.

7 Using a sponge and water, soak the paper on the front of the mosaic. Leave for 15 minutes.

8 Lift one corner of the paper to see if it comes away cleanly. If it does, peel the paper off carefully. If it proves difficult, leave it to soak a little longer and then try lifting it again.

9 Wipe away any surplus glue. Re-grout the plaque, including the sides. Remove excess grout with a damp sponge, then polish the surface with a dry, lint-free cloth.

This lantern is made by using a plain drinking glass as the base for a mosaic of tiny stained-glass squares, applied around the outside – a good way to use up glasses you're not too fond of.

Mosaic Lantern

You will need

indelible black felt-tipped pen

metal straightedge

pieces of stained glass: blue, green, red and yellow

glass cutter

ultraviolet glue

heavy-based glass tumbler

spatula and bowl

tile grout

black acrylic paint

sponge scourer

night-light

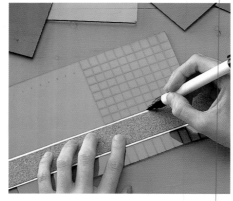

1 Using an indelible black felt-tipped pen and a metal straightedge, mark a neat grid of squares on each of the different coloured pieces of stained glass. Each square needs to measure 1cm/⅜in.

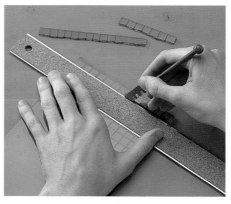

2 Cut the glass into 1cm/⅜in-lengths by scoring the glass with a glass cutter, using the straightedge as a guide. Tap underneath the score line with the ball end of the glass cutter, and then snap the glass apart gently between both thumbs.

3 Score the glass strip into 1cm/⅜in squares. Turn the strip over so the score lines face the worktop and tap each score line with the ball end of the glass cutter. The glass should break easily into squares.

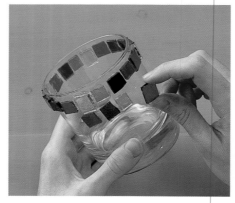

4 Using ultraviolet glue, stick the glass mosaic pieces around the glass tumbler, working from the top to the bottom. Leave a gap of 2mm/1⁄16in between squares to allow for grouting.

5 In a bowl, mix 30ml/2 tbsp of tile grout with 25ml/1½ tbsp of cold water and a 5cm/2in length of black acrylic paint. Stir until it forms a smooth, dark grey paste.

6 Using a spatula, press the grout into the gaps between the mosaic pieces. Remove any excess with the spatula, then allow to dry.

7 When the grout is dry, use a damp sponge scourer to clean any remaining smears of grout from the surface of the mosaic pieces.

8 When the lantern is clean, place a night-light in it. Never leave burning candles unattended and always keep them out of the reach of children.

Personal letters and correspondence often have a tendency to be lost or misplaced in a busy household. This simple design for a letter rack could be the solution.

Love Letter Rack

You will need

3mm/¹⁄₈in and 1.5cm/¹⁄₂in MDF (medium-density fibreboard) or plywood

pencil

jigsaw

PVA (white) glue

paintbrushes

wood glue

panel pins (narrow-headed nails)

pin hammer

vitreous glass tesserae

tile nippers

white cellulose filler

grout spreader or flexible knife

sponge

sandpaper

red acrylic paint

1 Draw the shapes of the components of the rack on to both pieces of MDF (medium-density fibreboard) or plywood. Cut them out with a jigsaw. Prime the surfaces with diluted PVA (white) glue. When dry, draw the pattern on to the front panel. Stick the pieces together with wood glue and secure with panel pins. Leave to dry overnight.

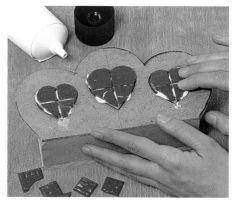

2 Select two tones of red vitreous glass tesserae to tile the heart motifs. Using tile nippers, nibble the tesserae into precise shapes to fit your design. Fix the tesserae in position on the front panel of the letter rack with white cellulose filler.

3 Select the colours of vitreous glass to tile around the hearts. Trim the tesserae to fit snugly around the heart motif and within the edges of the letter rack. Fix them to the base. Leave the rack to dry overnight.

4 Smooth more filler over the mosaic using a grout spreader or flexible knife. Rub the filler into all of the gaps with your fingers. Rub off any excess filler with a damp sponge and leave to dry.

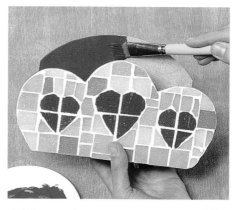

5 Use sandpaper to remove any filler that has dried on the surface of the mosaic and to neaten the edges. Paint the parts of the letter rack that are not covered with mosaic with red acrylic paint. Leave to dry.

A plain terracotta pot is decorated with squares of brightly coloured tesserae and mirror glass, set in white tile adhesive. This project is very simple to do – you could decorate several matching pots.

Jazzy Plant Pot

You will need

small terracotta plant pot
yacht varnish
paintbrush
vitreous glass tesserae
tile nippers
mirror glass
white cement-based tile adhesive
mixing bowl
flexible knife
sponge
sandpaper
soft cloth

1 Paint the inside of the plant pot with yacht varnish. Leave to dry. Cut the tesserae into neat quarters using tile nippers. Cut small squares of mirror glass the same size, also with tile nippers. Continue cutting the tesserae until you have enough pieces, in a variety of colours, to cover your pot completely.

2 Mix a quantity of tile adhesive as recommended by the manufacturer. Working from the bottom of the pot, spread a thick layer over a small area at a time using a flexible knife. Press the tesserae into the tile adhesive in rows, including the pieces of mirror glass. Leave to dry overnight.

3 Mix some more tile adhesive and rub all over the surface of the mosaic. Fill any gaps in between the tesserae, then wipe off excess adhesive with a damp sponge before it dries. Again, leave to dry overnight.

4 Use sandpaper to remove any lumps of tile adhesive that may have dried on to the surface of the tesserae, and to neaten the bottom edge of the pot.

5 Mix some more tile adhesive and smooth it all over the rim of the pot. Leave until completely dry, and then polish the finished mosaic well with a soft cloth.

This design relies on the various effects that are created by the juxtaposition of colours and textures. It can quite easily be adapted but should be kept simple for the best effect.

Mosaic Bottle

You will need
wine bottle
silicone sealant
pencil or pointed stick
vitreous glass tesserae, including white
tile nippers
cement-based tile adhesive
mixing container
soft cloth
sandpaper (optional)

1 Clean the bottle, rub off the label and dry thoroughly. Dab silicone sealant on to the bottle using a pencil or pointed stick to form a simple line drawing, such as a series of swirls.

2 Cut white vitreous glass into small pieces, about 2mm/$\frac{1}{16}$in and 4mm/$\frac{1}{8}$in, using tile nippers. Stick these tesserae to the lines drawn in silicone sealant, then leave overnight to dry.

3 Choose an assortment of colours from the vitreous glass and cut them into quarters. Some of the quarters will have to be cut across the diagonal, so that they can fit snugly between the white swirls. Stick these to the bottle in a series of bands of colour with the sealant. Leave overnight to dry.

4 Mix up some cement-based tile adhesive and rub the cement into the surface of the bottle. Make sure all the crevices between the tesserae are filled, otherwise the tesserae are liable to pull away, as the silicone sealant will remain rubbery. Wipe off excess cement with a dry soft cloth and leave overnight to dry.

5 If any of the tile adhesive has dried on to the surface of the tesserae, sand the bottle down. For a really smooth and glossy finish, polish the bottle with a dry soft cloth.

In this project, vitreous glass mosaic tiles in striking colours are used to decorate a ready-made fire screen. Most of this design uses whole tiles, cut diagonally into triangles.

Mosaic Fire Screen

You will need

ready-made fire-screen base

pencil

ruler

sharp knife

PVA (white) glue

paintbrushes

vitreous glass tesserae

tile nippers

ready-mixed tile grout

nailbrush

wood primer

white undercoat

gloss paint

soft cloth

1 Draw the design on to the surface of the screen and its feet. Calculate the space needed to accommodate the tiles required and mark the main areas with a ruler. Score the whole of the surface with a sharp knife, then prime with diluted PVA (white) glue and leave to dry completely.

2 Select a range of vitreous glass tiles in the colours you require. Use tile nippers to cut some of the tiles into right-angled triangles to use for the inner border design.

3 Stick the tesserae to the base with PVA glue. Try to make all the gaps between the tesserae equal and leave the area that will be slotted into the feet untiled.

4 Tile the edge, then the feet, making sure they will still slot on to the screen. Leave overnight to dry. Rub grout into the entire surface of the mosaic, making sure all the gaps between the tesserae are filled.

5 Leave the grout to dry for about ten minutes, then remove any excess with a nailbrush. Allow to dry for a further 12 hours, then paint the back of the screen with wood primer, then undercoat and finally gloss paint, allowing each coat to dry before you apply the next. Finally, polish the mosaic with a soft cloth and slot on the feet.

This mosaic jewellery box was inspired by the treasures of the Aztecs and Mayas of pre-Colombian Central America, which were decorated with turquoise, coral and jade.

Aztec Box

You will need

wooden box with hinged lid

felt-tipped pen or dark pencil

glass nuggets backed with gold and silver leaf

PVA (white) glue

glue brush

masking tape

mixing container

fine artist's paintbrush

vitreous glass tesserae

tile nippers

cinca ceramic tiles

sand

cement

black cement dye

sponge

soft cloth

plastic bag

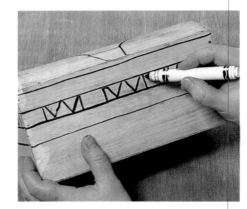

1 Draw the design on the wooden box with a felt-tipped pen or dark pencil. The design represents the head of a fierce animal, and the teeth and jaws of the beast are drawn immediately below the opening edge of the lid, using the picture as a guide.

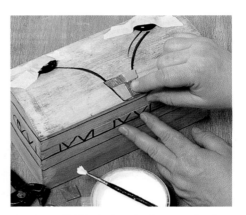

2 Using PVA (white) glue, stick glass nuggets on the box for the eyes. Hold them in place with masking tape to dry. Cut vitreous glass tiles in coral and stick on to the nose and lips. Cut vitreous glass tiles in terracotta and pink for the lips. Use a paintbrush to apply glue to small pieces.

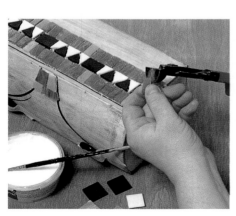

3 Cut triangular black and white tesserae into precise shapes to fit the areas marked for the teeth, then stick them in place.

4 Select tesserae in varying shades and use to define the eye sockets and the snout, cutting to fit as necessary. Include a few small nuggets positioned randomly. When tiling around the hinges, leave 1cm/½in untiled, so the box can be opened. Leave it to dry, then tile the lid in the same way.

5 Mix three parts sand with one part cement. Add some black cement dye. Add water, mixing it to the desired consistency. Rub the cement on to the box surface. Scrape off the excess, rub the box with a slightly damp sponge and polish with a dry cloth. Cover with plastic to dry slowly.

In this ambitious project the mosaic is arranged on a clear glass base. Place the screen in front of a window so that the light shines through, making the colours of the stained glass glow.

Stained-glass Screen

You will need
mitre block
hacksaw
tape measure
3 pieces of 2.5cm/1in x 3.5cm/1½in wood, each 206cm/81in long, with a 1cm/½in rebate
wood glue
hammer
12 corner staples
pencil
hand drill
4 small hinges
screwdriver and screws
large sheet of paper
indelible felt-tipped pen
3 pieces of clear glass, each 70 x 25cm/27½ x 10in
glass cutter
7 pieces of coloured glass, 27cm/10½in square
clear all-purpose adhesive
tile grout
universal black stain
mixing bowl
old toothbrush
paint scraper
soft cloths
3 pieces of rectangular beading, each 2m/79in long
panel pins (brads)
12 metal corner plates

1 Using a mitre block and a hacksaw, cut two pieces of rebated wood 74cm/ 29in long, and two 29cm/11½in long from each length for the frame. Arrange the wood into three frames. Glue the mitred ends together with wood glue, checking that they are at right angles. Leave to dry, then hammer in a corner staple at each corner.

2 Place one frame on top of another, with the rebates facing outwards. With a pencil, mark the position of two small hinges and their screwholes on two adjacent side edges of the frames. Drill a shallow guidehole for each screw, then screw in the hinges. Attach the third frame in the same way.

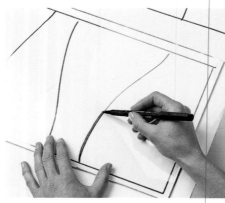

3 Place the three frames face down on a sheet of paper. Using a felt-tipped pen, draw around the inner edge of each frame. Draw a design that flows in bands across the frames. Centre the pieces of clear glass over the drawing. Trace the design on to the glass.

4 Using a glass cutter, cut 12 right-angled triangles of coloured glass for the corners of the screen and set aside. Cut the rest randomly.

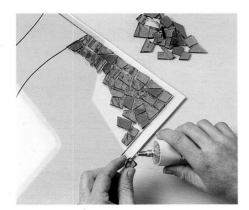

5 Using clear adhesive, glue the coloured glass pieces on to the clear glass panels. Work on a section of your design at a time, following each band across to the other panels. Leave to dry for 2 hours.

6 Mix the tile grout with the black stain and rub it over the surface of the mosaic. Use a toothbrush to fill all the gaps. Leave to dry for 1 hour.

7 When completely dry, clean off the excess grout. Residual, stubborn grout can be removed carefully with a paint scraper. Finish removing any smaller areas of grout with a soft cloth.

8 Glue one of the reserved right-angled triangles of coloured glass over the corner of the frame, at the front. Repeat with the other triangles on each corner of the frame.

9 Cut each piece of beading into two lengths each 71cm/28in and two lengths each 23cm/9in. Put the glass panels in the frames, slot the beading behind them and fix them in place with panel pins (brads).

10 Make shallow guideholes with a hand drill, then screw the corner plates to the back of each corner of the frame. Finally polish the surface of your mosaic screen with a soft cloth.

Give your bathroom a new lease of life with this colourful and original fish splashback. Beads clustered together make an original addition to mosaics, and are perfect for creating intricate shapes.

Fish Splashback

You will need

pencil

paper

piece of plywood to fit splashback area

carbon paper

vitreous glass tesserae in a variety of colours

wood glue

interior filler

mixing container

spoon

acrylic paints in a variety of colours

selection of beads including:

metallic bugle beads,

frosted and metallic square beads,

large round beads and mixed beads

tile nippers

tile grout

cloth

1 Sketch the design to fit the splashback on a large sheet of paper, keeping the shapes simple and bold. Use a sheet of carbon paper to transfer the design to the plywood by drawing firmly over all the lines using a pencil.

2 Apply the mosaic border. Lay out all the tiles first, alternating the colours. Then apply wood glue to the border, a small section at a time, positioning the tiles carefully on top of the glue as you work along.

4 Spread green filler thickly over the seaweed fronds, then carefully press in metallic green bugle beads. Fill in the fish fins using green filler and metallic green square beads. Make sure all the beads are on their sides so that the holes do not show.

5 Mix up another small amount of interior filler, this time colouring it with the orange acrylic paint. Spread filler thickly over the starfish and press in orange square frosted beads. Use some darker beads for shading.

3 Following the manufacturer's instructions, mix up a small amount of interior filler, then add some green acrylic paint to colour it.

6 Glue on a large bead for the fish eye using wood glue. Mix up some white filler and spread it thickly on to a 5cm/2in-square section of the fish body and press in mixed beads. Repeat, working in small sections, until the fish is complete.

7 Glue on large beads for bubbles. For the background design and the rocks at the bottom of the splash back, use mosaic tile nippers to cut the mosaic tiles into 1cm/½in squares.

8 Fill in the background, varying the shades and sticking the tiles down with wood glue. Clip the edges of the tiles to fit any curves. Mix up some tile grout following the manufacturer's instructions and spread over the design. Spread lightly and carefully over the beaded areas. Wipe off with a damp cloth and leave to dry.

This design is simple to execute and adds a naive charm to a plain wooden tray. The semi-indirect method of mosaic used here helps to keep the surface smooth and flat.

Country Cottage Tray

You will need

scissors

brown paper

wooden tray

pencil

tracing paper (optional)

tile nippers

vitreous glass tesserae

water-soluble glue

white spirit (paint thinner)

PVA (white) glue

mixing container

old household paintbrush

bradawl (with chisel edge) or other sharp instrument

masking tape

cement-based tile adhesive

notched spreader

sponge

soft cloth

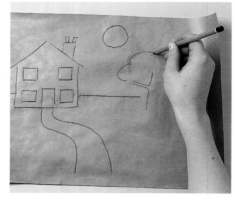

1 Cut a piece of brown paper to fit the bottom of the wooden tray. Draw a very simple picture in pencil or trace the template at the back of the book. Plan out the colour scheme for the picture and, using the tile nippers cut all of the vitreous glass tesserae into quarters.

2 Position the tiles on to the paper to check your design before going any further. Once you are satisfied with the design, apply water-soluble glue on to the paper in small areas, and stick the tiles on face down. Take care to obscure any pencil marks. Trim the tiles to fit if necessary.

3 Prepare the bottom of the tray by removing any varnish or polish with white spirit (paint thinner). Prime with diluted PVA (white) glue, leave it to dry, then score it with a sharp instrument such as a bradawl. Protect the sides with masking tape.

4 Mix the tile adhesive according to the manufacturer's instructions. Spread an even layer over the bottom of the tray, using a notched spreader. Cover the tray completely and spread well into the corners.

5 Place the mosaic carefully in the freshly-applied tile adhesive, paper side up. Press down firmly over the whole surface, then leave for about 30 minutes. Moisten the paper with a damp sponge and peel off. Leave the tile adhesive to dry overnight.

6 Some parts of the mosaic may need to be grouted with extra tile adhesive. Leave it to dry, then clean off any of the adhesive that may have dried on the surface with a sponge. Remove the pieces of masking tape and then polish the mosaic with a soft cloth.

Create your own abstract mirror frame using the semi-indirect method. This design features a colourful mixture of shapes in varying sizes. Copy it or use it as a basis for your own creation.

Abstract Mirror

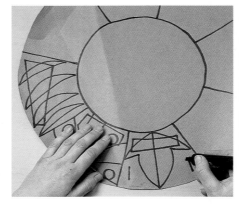

1 Draw a circle on brown paper 2mm/1/16 in smaller than the board using a pair of compasses, and cut it out. Place the mirror in the centre and draw around it in black pen. Divide the border into eight equal sections. Draw a design clearly in each section.

2 Place the mirror face down in the centre of the paper and attach it with a curl of masking tape. Cut all the tesserae to size with the tile nippers. Stick them face down on to the paper design, using water-soluble glue. Keep the gaps between the tesserae even.

3 When the tile design is complete, carefully lower the mosaic on to the board and attach the lip around the outside. Remove the mirror and cut away the brown paper underneath it using a craft knife.

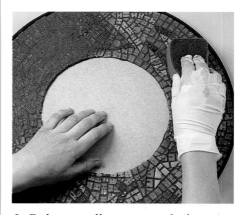

4 Rub a small amount of tile grout into the mosaic, then wipe off the excess with a damp sponge. This will bind the tesserae together. Leave it until the grout is almost dry.

5 Gently remove the mosaic from the board by turning the board upside down. Spread the outer area of the board with tile adhesive using a notched spreader. Press the mosaic into it firmly, tile side down.

6 Coat the back of the mirror with the silicone-based adhesive and stick it into the centre of the board. Leave to set for 20 minutes.

7 Dampen the paper with a sponge, wait 10 minutes, then gently peel it off the mosaic. Clean away any lumps of cement with a damp sponge. Leave to dry then re-grout the mosaic, filling in any cracks, and sponge clean.

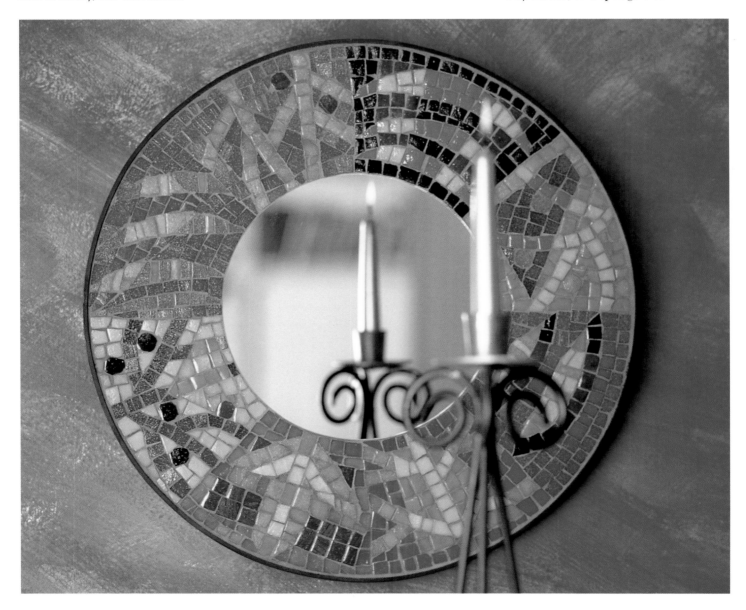

This lovely mosaic table provides a stunning focal point for any room in the home. With its swirling pattern, the mosaic evokes fresh sea breezes sweeping in off the water.

Mosaic Table

You will need
piece of plywood
jigsaw
sharp knife
PVA (white) glue
paintbrushes
pencil
tile nippers
vitreous glass tesserae, in various colours
cement-based tile adhesive powder
soft brush
plastic spray bottle
cloths
fine sandpaper

1 Cut the plywood to the desired shape for your table. Score it with a sharp knife and prime it with a coat of diluted PVA (white) glue. Leave to dry thoroughly.

2 For the table design pictured here, use a pencil to draw a series of swirls radiating from the centre of the table. If you prefer, create your own design.

3 Use tile nippers to cut white glass tiles into quarters, and use different densities of white to add interest to the finished design.

4 Brush PVA glue along the pencil line swirls, then position the white glass tiles on top of the layer of glue, smooth side up.

5 Select your colours for the areas between the white lines. Here, browns and sand colours form the edge while blues, greens and whites are used for the central areas. Spread out your selected colours to see whether the combinations work.

6 Using the tile nippers, cut all of the coloured squares you have chosen into quarters.

7 Glue the central pieces to the table-top with PVA glue. To finish off the edge, glue pieces around the border of the table to match the design of the top surface. Leave the glue to dry thoroughly overnight.

8 Sprinkle dry cement-based tile adhesive over the mosaic and spread it with a brush, filling all the spaces. Spray with water wetting all of the cement. Wipe away any excess.

9 Mix up some tile adhesive with water and rub it into the edges of the table with your fingers. Leave it to dry overnight.

10 Rub off any excess cement with fine sandpaper and finish the table by polishing the mosaic thoroughly with a soft cloth.

This unusual garden urn is decorated with modern faces but has a look that is reminiscent of Byzantine icons. A simple and naive drawing of a face can look better than realistic depictions when rendered in mosaic.

Garden Urn

You will need

large frost-resistant urn

yacht varnish

paintbrush

chalk

vitreous glass tesserae

tile nippers

cement-based tile adhesive

mixing container

flexible knife

sponge

sandpaper

dilute hydrochloric acid (optional)

1 Paint the inside of the urn with yacht varnish, then leave to dry. Divide the pot into quarters and draw your design on each quarter with chalk. The design used here depicts four different heads and shoulders. Keep the drawing simple, sketching just the basic elements of the face.

2 Choose a dark colour from the range of tiles for the main outlines and details such as eyes and lips. Cut these into eighths using tile nippers. Mix up cement-based tile adhesive and stick the tesserae on to your drawing lines. Select a range of shades for the flesh tones and cut into quarters.

3 Working on a small area at a time, apply cement-based tile adhesive to the face and press the tesserae into it. Use a mixture of all the colours, but in areas of shade use more of the darker tesserae and in highlighted areas use more of the lighter pieces.

4 Choose colours for the area that surrounds the heads. Spread these out on a clean table to see if they work together. A mixture of blues and whites with a little green has been chosen here. Cut the pieces into quarters with tile nippers.

5 Working on a small area at a time, spread tile adhesive on to the surface and press the cut vitreous glass into it, making sure the colours are arranged randomly. Cover the outer surface of the urn with tesserae, then leave to dry for 24 hours.

6 Mix up more tile adhesive and spread it all over the surface of the mosaic. Do this thoroughly, making sure you fill all the gaps between the tesserae. This is especially important if the urn is going to be put outside. Wipe off any excess cement with a sponge and leave to dry for 24 hours.

7 Use sandpaper to remove any cement that has dried on the surface of the mosaic. If the cement is hard to remove, dilute hydrochloric acid can be used. Wear protective clothing and a mask. Wash any acid residue from the surface with plenty of water and leave the urn to dry.

8 Finish off the urn by rubbing some more of the tile adhesive over the lip and around the inside rim of the pot. This will prevent the mosaic design from seeming to end too abruptly and will give the urn and mosaic a more unified appearance.

Ceramic Mosaic

Ceramic mosaic differs from glass mosaic in the materials used to make it, otherwise the techniques are exactly the same. Ceramic kitchen and bathroom tiles, and china can all be used to create ceramic mosaics as well as purpose-made ceramic tiles. As tiles and china do not break into regular and even-size pieces, ceramic mosaic can have the appearance of crazy paving, which adds to the decorative effect.

Miniature Crazy Paving

There is a lot more scope in the materials you can use with ceramic mosaic than with glass mosaic. In addition to using plain and patterned household tiles, you can use broken pieces of china including all those bits you dig up in the garden. Try scouring junk shops and market stalls for pieces of old china. Ceramic mosaic offers a fantastic opportunity to recycle favourite china that has been accidentally smashed.

One of the challenges of working with ceramics is smashing china into usable size and shaped tesserae needed for the mosaics, while keeping the

patterned area you want centred in the shards. Simply wrap each piece of china or each tile in a piece of sacking (heavy cloth) to prevent shards from flying everywhere, and then smash it with a hammer. The result will be irreg-

ular-size pieces of ceramic which you can either "nibble" further with tile nippers to make the shapes you want, or use as they are. The technique for ceramic mosaic is the same as for glass mosaic, so follow the techniques for that chapter.

Blue and white patterned china works well in mosaic, but try other combinations for different decorative effects. One possible disadvantage of using ceramics over glass tesserae is that you might not have enough of the colour or pattern you want,

particularly if you have collected pieces from junk shops. It is always wise, therefore, to check before starting a piece that you have enough of a colour, rather than running out halfway through.

This chapter features creative projects for decorative wall panels and plaques, mirrors, vases, and even a crazy paving chair to inspire your creativity. Start with something simple, such as a wall plaque

or outdoor pot and work your way up to tackle a more complicated project. Alternatively, you could go off on a tangent and decorate shelves, table tops, door panels, and any other surface you desire, in your own mosaic designs. Remember, however,

that mosaic is very heavy, so the base must be solid enough to be able to withstand the combined weight of china and grout.

Fragments of plain and patterned broken tile have been incorporated into the design of these plant pots. Collect your materials by looking in junk shops for old china in contrasting and complementary patterns.

Plant Pots

You will need

terracotta flower pots

PVA (white) glue and brush (optional)

mixing container

acrylic paint

paintbrush

chalk or wax crayon

plain and patterned ceramic tiles

tile nippers

rubber (latex) gloves

flexible knife

tile adhesive

powdered waterproof tile grout

cement dye

cloth

nailbrush

lint-free, soft cloth

1 If the pots are not frost-resistant and they are intended for outdoor use, treat inside and out by sealing with a coat of diluted PVA (white) glue. Allow to dry. Paint the inside of all the pots with acrylic paint in your chosen colour. Leave to dry. Using chalk or a wax crayon, roughly sketch out the design for the tile pieces.

2 Snip small pieces of ceramic tile to fit within your chosen design. Using a flexible knife, spread tile adhesive on to small areas of the design at a time. Press the tile pieces in place, working on the outlines first, and then filling in the background.

3 Mix powdered grout with water and a little cement dye. Spread the grout over the pot, filling all the cracks between the tile pieces. Allow the surface to dry thoroughly.

4 Brush off any excess with a nail-brush. Allow to dry thoroughly for at least 48 hours, and then polish with a dry, soft cloth.

This sunflower mosaic is simple to make and, if you have enough china, you could make several plaques to brighten up an outdoor wall. Collect bright fragments of china in a harmonious blend of colours.

Sunflower Mosaic

You will need

pencil

5mm/¼in thick plywood sheet

coping saw or fretsaw

medium- and fine-grade sandpaper

bradawl

electric cable

wire cutters

masking tape

PVA (white) glue, diluted

white undercoat paint

paintbrush

tile nippers

china fragments

mirror glass strips

tile adhesive

grout

mixing container

cement dye

nailbrush

soft cloth

1 Draw a simple sunflower on the plywood. Cut it out with a saw and sand any rough edges. Make two holes in the plywood with a bradawl. Strip the cable and cut a short length of wire. Push the ends of the wire through the holes from the back and fix the ends with masking tape at the front. Seal the front with the diluted PVA (white) glue. Seal the back with white undercoat paint.

2 Using tile nippers, cut the china and mirror strips into irregular shapes. Stick them to the plywood using tile adhesive. Dip each fragment in the tile adhesive and scoop up enough of it to cover the sticking surface; the tile adhesive needs to squelch out around the edge of the mosaic to make sure that it adheres securely. Leave the adhesive to dry thoroughly overnight.

3 Mix up the grout with cement dye, as directed by the manufacturer. Press a small amount of wet grout into the gaps on the mosaic. Leave to dry for about 5 minutes. Brush off any excess with a nailbrush. Leave again for 5 minutes and then polish well with a clean, soft cloth. Leave overnight to dry.

These mosaic spheres can be used as unusual garden ornaments, or a bowlful could make a striking table centrepiece. Select fragments of china to complement your tableware or garden.

Decorative Spheres

You will need

10 polystyrene or wooden spheres

PVA (white) glue

paintbrush

pencil

selection of china

mirror glass

tile nippers

waterproof tile adhesive

powdered tile grout

mixing container

vinyl matt emulsion (flat latex) or acrylic paint

nailbrush

soft cloth

1 Seal the polystyrene or wooden spheres with diluted PVA (white) glue. Leave to dry. Roughly draw a simple design on to each sphere using a pencil. A combination of circular motifs and stripes works well, but you can experiment with other geometric shapes and abstract designs.

2 Cut your china and mirror into pieces using the tile nippers. Combine different sizes of tesserae to fit the design. Stick them to the spheres with a waterproof tile adhesive. Leave to dry overnight.

3 Mix grout with water and a little coloured vinyl matt emulsion (flat latex) or acrylic paint. Rub the grout into the surface of each sphere, filling all of the cracks between the tesserae.

4 Leave for a few minutes until the surface has dried, then brush off any excess grout using a stiff nailbrush.

5 Leave to dry overnight, then polish with a dry soft cloth. Allow the spheres to air for a few days before you arrange them.

If you would like to introduce mosaic to an outdoor setting but are daunted by a large project, these tiles are the perfect solution. They could be fixed to a wall as an interesting feature.

China Tiles

You will need
plain white tiles
PVA (white) glue
paintbrush
pencil
tile nippers
selection of china
tile adhesive
mixing container
acrylic paint or cement dye
powdered waterproof tile grout
nailbrush
soft cloth

1 Prime the back of a plain tile with diluted PVA (white) glue and leave to dry. Draw a simple, rough design on the back of the tile using a pencil.

2 Using tile nippers, cut a selection of china into small pieces that will fit into your design and arrange these in groups according to their colour and shape.

3 Dip the tesserae into tile adhesive and press them, one by one, on to the tile, using the drawing as a guide. Make sure there is enough adhesive on the tesserae; when they are pressed on the tile, glue should ooze out around the tesserae. When the tile is covered, leave it to dry overnight.

4 Mix acrylic paint or cement dye with powdered waterproof tile grout. Add water and mix to a dough-like consistency. Rub the grout into the surface of the mosaic, making sure all the gaps between the tesserae are filled. Leave to dry for 10 minutes.

5 Scrub the surface of the tile with a stiff nailbrush to remove all the excess grout, which should come away as powder. When clean, leave the tile to dry for 24 hours. Finish by polishing it with a soft cloth.

A simple spiral was the inspiration for this tall, elegant lamp base. Pieces of mirror have been added to catch the light, and they sparkle when the lamp is switched on.

Spiral Lamp Stand

You will need

pencil

cardboard carpet roll tube

5mm/¼in plywood

jigsaw

drill and bit

bradawl

length of electric flex

wood glue

shellac

household paintbrushes

hollow metal rod with a screw thread, the length of the finished stand

plaster of Paris

mixing container

ceramic tiles in three colours

tile nippers

cement-based tile adhesive

sponge

mirror glass

flexible knife

sandpaper

soft cloth

copper tubing

hacksaw

lamp fittings

plug

screwdriver

lampshade

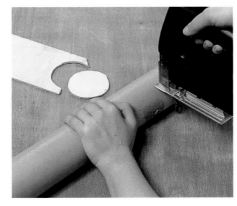

1 Draw twice around the circular end of the cardboard tube on to the plywood. Cut around these circles using a jigsaw and cut the cardboard tube to the length required. Drill a hole through the centre of one of the plywood circles. Use a bradawl to make a hole in the cardboard tube 2cm/¾in from one end and big enough to take the electric flex.

2 Use wood glue to stick the plywood circle without the drilled hole to the end of the tube with the flex hole. Leave to dry overnight, then paint the cardboard tube with shellac. Thread the flex through the hole in the tube and the hollow metal rod. Stand the metal rod inside the tube with the screw thread at the top.

◄ **3** Mix some plaster of Paris with water and quickly pour it into the tube. Slip the second plywood circle over the metal rod and secure it with wood glue to the top of the cardboard tube. As soon as you have poured the plaster of Paris into the tube, you must work quickly to secure the top, as it is very important that the plaster dries with the rod in the upright position. Leave overnight to dry.

►

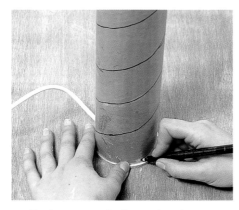

4 With a pencil, draw the design on to the tube, following the spiral lines that are already present on the cardboard tube. You can add variations and embellishments at this stage.

5 Cut the tiles for the outline colour into small pieces using tile nippers. Stick these to the lines of your design using cement-based tile adhesive. Use a sponge to wipe away any large blobs of cement that seep out from under the tesserae, and then leave to dry overnight.

6 Select two colours of tile to fill the areas between the spiralling lines. Use the tile nippers to cut the tiles into various shapes and sizes, then cut the mirror into various shapes and sizes.

7 Spread cement-based tile adhesive on to the remaining cardboard area, and apply the tesserae in separate bands of colour. Work on a small area at a time, so that the surface does not become too messy. Intersperse the coloured tesserae with pieces of mirror as you work. Cover the whole of the cardboard tube, and then leave it to dry overnight.

8 Using a flexible knife, apply wet cement-based tile adhesive over the whole area of the lamp stand, taking care to press it down between all the tesserae. Wipe off the excess cement with a sponge and leave the stand to dry overnight. Rub off any excess surface cement with sandpaper, and polish with a soft cloth.

9 Finish off by attaching all of the fittings. Slip copper tubing, cut to size, over the central rod, leaving the screw end exposed. Attach the lamp fittings, plug, and lampshade.

The undulating, fractured surface of the frame sets off the smooth, reflective plane of the glass perfectly. It is made from pieces of very delicately patterned china in cool, fresh colours with touches of gold.

Arched Mirror

You will need

2cm/¾in plywood

pencil

ruler

jigsaw

sandpaper

PVA (white) glue

paintbrushes

wood primer

white undercoat

gloss paint

drill with rebating bit

mirror plate

2 x 2cm/¾in screws

screwdriver

thick cardboard

scissors

3mm/⅛in foil-backed mirror

ready-mixed tile adhesive

flexible knife

masking tape

tracing paper (optional)

tile nippers

selection of china

powdered tile grout

vinyl matt emulsion (flat latex) or acrylic paint (optional)

mixing container

grout spreader or rubber (latex) gloves

nailbrush

soft cloth

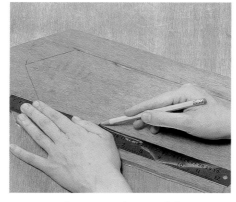

1 Draw the outer shape of the mirror frame on to plywood. Cut around this shape using a jigsaw, then sand down the rough edges. On to this base panel, draw the desired shape of the mirror glass. Here, the shape of the glass echoes the shape of the panel, but it can also be a completely different shape if desired. Make sure it is a shape that glass-cutters will be able to reproduce without difficulty.

2 Seal the sides and front of the base panel with diluted PVA (white) glue and paint the back first with wood primer, then undercoat and finally gloss paint. Mark the position of the mirror plate on the back. Using the right bit, rebate the area that will be under the keyhole-shaped opening (large enough to take a screw head). Then screw the mirror plate in place.

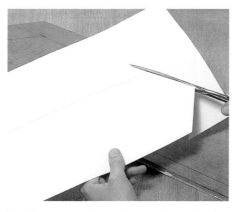

3 Cut a cardboard template in the exact dimensions of the mirror shape you have drawn on the base. Ask your supplier to cut a piece of foil-backed mirror using your template.

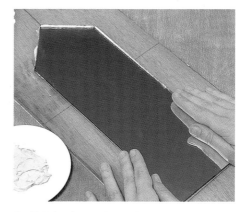

4 Stick the mirror in position using ready-mixed tile adhesive. Leave to dry overnight.

▶

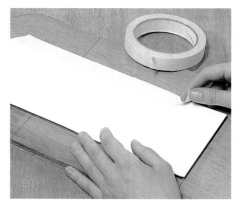

5 Trim 2mm/¹⁄₁₆in from the template all around the edge. Cover the mirror with it, securing it with masking tape; this should prevent the mirror from being scratched. The mosaic will eventually overlap the 2mm/¹⁄₁₆in of uncovered mirror.

6 Draw the design for the frame on the dry, sealed surface surrounding the mirror; use tracing paper and a soft pencil to copy and transfer the design from your original plan, if you wish.

7 Using tile nippers, snip the smooth edges from the cups and plates you have collected. Use these to tile the outside edge of the base panel and to overlap the 2mm/¹⁄₁₆in edges of the mirror, sticking them down with ready-mixed tile adhesive. Cut the remainder of the china into small pieces and stick these to the structural lines of your design.

8 Fill in the areas of detail between the outlining tesserae. When all the mirror frame has been tiled, leave to dry for 24 hours. Mix powdered tile grout with water and colour it with vinyl matt emulsion or acrylic paint, if you like.

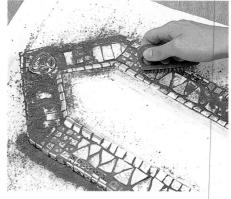

9 Spread the adhesive over the surface of the tesserae using a grout spreader or wear rubber (latex) gloves and rub it in by hand, making sure all the gaps between the tesserae have been filled. Allow to dry for a few minutes, then brush off the excess grout with a stiff-bristled nailbrush.

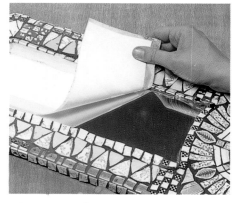

10 Wipe clean with a soft cloth. Leave overnight to dry thoroughly, then remove the protective cardboard from the mirrored glass and hang in position.

This delicate mosaic is made entirely from old cups and plates. This pretty trinket box is ideal for displaying on a dressing table, and can be used for storing jewellery, letters and other treasures.

Floral Trinket Box

You will need
wooden box
PVA (white) glue
mixing container
old household paintbrush
bradawl or other sharp instrument
soft dark pencil
tile nippers
white and patterned old china
cement-based tile adhesive
admix
flexible knife
cloths
paint scraper

1 Prime the top and sides of the wooden box with diluted PVA (white) glue. Leave to dry, then score it at random with a bradawl or other sharp implement to key the surface.

2 Using a soft pencil and the template at the back of the book, draw a grid on the box. Draw a flower in each square, with a large flower in the centre.

3 Cut the pieces of white china into small squares. Mix the tile adhesive with admix. Using a flexible knife, spread this along the grid lines, a small area at a time.

4 Press the white tesserae into the adhesive in neat, close-fitting rows. Cover all of the grid lines on the top and sides of the box. Leave it to dry completely overnight.

5 Using tile nippers, cut out small pieces of the patterned china. Sort them into colours. Position the tesserae on the box and plan out the colour scheme.

6 Spread the tile adhesive and admix over each square of the top and sides in turn. Press in the tesserae to make each flower and the background. Leave to dry.

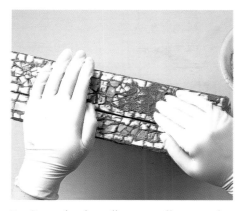

7 Spread tile adhesive all over the surface of the mosaic, getting right into the crevices and wiping off excess adhesive with a damp cloth.

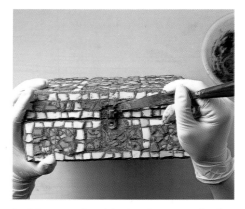

8 Using a flexible knife, smooth the tile adhesive around the hinges and clasp, if there is one. Remove any excess adhesive immediately with a cloth before it dries. Leave to dry.

9 Using a paint scraper, scrape off any tile adhesive that may have dried on the surface of the mosaic. Take care not to scratch the surface of the tiles.

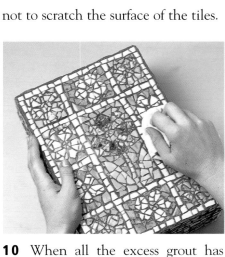

10 When all the excess grout has been removed, polish the surface of the box with a soft cloth, rubbing each tile fragment to a high shine.

Gently spiralling bands of mosaic look very elegant on a tall shaped vase. The top and base of the vase are given a marble finish to enclose the rest of the mosaic.

Spiral Vase

You will need

tall vase

paintbrush (optional)

yacht varnish (optional)

white chalk

marble tile

piece of sacking (heavy cloth)

hammer

cement-based tile adhesive

mixing container

flexible knife

pale blue and royal blue, glazed

ceramic tiles

gold smalti

tile nippers

notched spreader or cloth pad

sandpaper

soft cloth

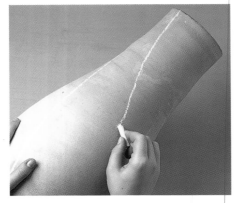

1 If your vase is unglazed, seal it by painting all around the inside top lip with yacht varnish. Using a piece of white chalk, draw lines spiralling gently from the rim of the vase to the base. Make sure you have an even number of bands and that they are regularly spaced.

2 Wrap the marble tile in sacking (heavy cloth), then break it up using a hammer. Mix up the tile adhesive following the manufacturer's instructions. Using a flexible knife, spread a thin band around the top and bottom of the vase, press in the marble pieces and leave to dry overnight.

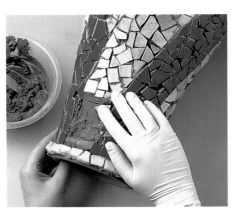

3 Using a hammer and sacking, break up all the pale blue and royal blue tiles. Spread tile adhesive over the vase, a band at a time, and press in the tesserae, alternating the two colours. Leave to dry, preferably overnight.

4 Use the tile nippers to cut the gold smalti into small pieces. Using the knife, place blobs of adhesive in the larger gaps between the blue tesserae. Press the gold smalti pieces at random over the blue spirals, checking that they are all level with the rest of the tiles. Leave to dry overnight.

5 Using a notched spreader or cloth pad, rub more tile adhesive in the colour of your choice, over the surface of the mosaic, carefully filling all the gaps. Wipe off the excess and leave to dry overnight. Sand off any adhesive dried on the surface, then polish with a clean, soft cloth.

A mosaic splashback makes a very practical surface above a sink, as it is strong and durable as well as waterproof. This jaunty boat design is made entirely from broken tile mosaic.

Boat Splashback

You will need

1.5cm/½in plywood, cut to the desired size

PVA (white) glue

paintbrush

craft knife

pencil

work bench and clamps

bradawl

plain, glazed ceramic tiles: red, pale blue, dark blue and white

piece of heavy sacking

hammer

tile nippers

old knife or flexible spreader

cement-based tile adhesive

white, glazed ceramic tile border strip

mirror tiles

sponge

scissors

plastic drinking straw

sanding block

lint-free cloth

yacht varnish and brush

1 Seal the front and back of the cut plywood with diluted PVA (white) glue. Leave it to dry, then score the front of the board with a craft knife.

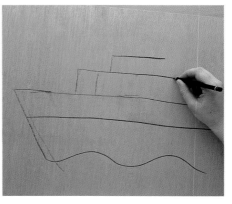

2 Draw a simple boat design on the front of the board. Place the board on a work bench, then clamp in position and use a bradawl to make a screw hole in each corner.

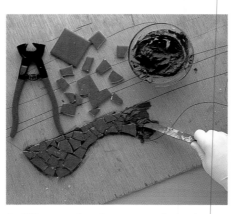

3 Wrap each tile separately in heavy sacking and break with a hammer. Trim the pieces with tile nippers if necessary. Using a knife or flexible spreader, spread tile adhesive within the lines of the drawing, then stick down the tesserae, as shown.

4 Build up the shape, leaving the portholes and windows blank. Fill in the background sea and sky with pale blue tile pieces. Continue to within 1cm/½in of the edge of the board, avoiding the screw holes.

5 Cut up the white border strip into short lengths with tile nippers. Fill in the border around the edge of the design, working as before, and leaving a gap between each border piece for grouting.

6 Add pieces of mirror tile to make the portholes and windows. Remove excess adhesive from the surface of the splashback with a damp sponge. Leave to dry for 24 hours. Push a length of drinking straw into each hole.

7 Spread more tile adhesive over the surface, covering any sharp edges. Smooth the adhesive around the straws. Remove excess adhesive with a damp sponge, then leave the splashback to dry for 24 hours. Smooth the tile surface lightly with a sanding block, then polish with a dry, lint-free cloth. Seal the back of the board with two coats of yacht varnish, allowing it to dry between coats.

The daisy-filled panels of this pine bedhead would look beautiful in a country bedroom with distressed wooden furniture. Make a footboard to match or use the same design to decorate other panelled furniture.

Mosaic Bedhead

You will need

unvarnished pine bedhead and footboard
PVA (white) glue and brush
craft knife
old palette knife or flexible spreader
cement-based tile adhesive
admix
mixing container
soft pencil
plain, glazed ceramic tiles: white, orange, green and honey-coloured
piece of heavy sacking
hammer
tile nippers
rubber-edged spreader
lint-free cloth
sponge
sanding block

1 Seal the surface of the wood with PVA (white) glue. When dry, score the surface with a craft knife.

2 Using a palette knife or flexible spreader, fill any recesses in the areas to be decorated with the tile adhesive mixed with admix. Leave for 24 hours to allow the adhesive to set.

4 Wrap each white and orange tile separately in sacking and break them with a hammer. Trim the white tile pieces into petal shapes with the tile nippers. Trim the orange tile pieces into round centres for the daisies.

5 Spread tile adhesive over the daisy shapes on the panels. Press the white and orange mosaic pieces in place to make flowers.

3 Draw a daisy design on the panels with a soft pencil.

6 Smash the green tiles as before and shape the pieces with tile nippers to make stems and leaves. Spread the adhesive over the appropriate areas of the design, then press the green mosaic pieces into position.

7 Make all the leaves and stems, and then leave the tile adhesive to dry for 24 hours.

8 Smash the honey-coloured tiles as before. Spread tile adhesive around the daisies and fill in the background, cutting the pieces of tile as necessary so that they fit.

9 Using a rubber-edged spreader or lint-free cloth, spread adhesive over the mosaic, pushing it into the gaps and covering all the sharp corners. Remove excess with a damp sponge.

10 Leave the mosaic for 24 hours to dry, then lightly smooth the surface of the mosaic with a sanding block. Polish with a dry, lint-free cloth.

This striking table has been decorated with bits of broken china and chipped decorative tiles, yet with clever colour co-ordination and a very simple design, it makes an attractive piece of garden furniture.

Mosaic Garden Table

You will need

2.5cm/1in plywood, at least 122cm/4ft square

string

drawing (push) pin

pencil

jigsaw

wood primer

paintbrush

broken china

tile nippers

tile adhesive

mixing container

flexible knife

tile grout

grout colour (optional)

washing-up (dishwashing) brush

1 To mark a circle on the plywood, tie one end of a 60cm/2ft length of string to a drawing (push) pin. Tie a pencil to the other end. Push the pin into the centre of the plywood, then draw the circle. Cut it out using a jigsaw. Draw your chosen design on the plywood circle, adjusting the string length to draw concentric circles.

2 Prime the plywood circle with wood primer on the front, back and around the edge. Apply a thick and even coat, and allow each side to dry before proceeding with the next. Allow the primer to dry thoroughly according to the manufacturer's instructions before proceeding further.

3 Snip pieces of the border china to fit your chosen design and arrange them on the table top.

4 Mix up the tile adhesive according to the manufacturer's instructions and spread it on to the back of each piece of china with a flexible knife before fixing it in position. Cover the whole table with the design.

5 Mix up the grout and colour it as desired, then work it into all the gaps. Using a washing-up (dishwashing) brush, continue to work the grout in, then clean off any excess.

This decorative work is made with handpainted Mexican tiles, which are widely available. The blue and white patterned tesserae make a lively background, and the tree trunk is simply the back of the tiles.

Tree of Life Wall Panel

You will need

2cm/¾in plywood, cut to the size
required – adjust your measurements
to fit a row of whole border tiles
in each direction

pencil

hand drill

mirror plate

screwdriver

15mm/½in screws

PVA (white) glue

mixing container

old household paintbrush

bradawl or other sharp implement

small, handpainted, glazed
ceramic tiles

tape measure

soft dark pencil

tracing paper (optional)

tile nippers

blue and white, handpainted, glazed
ceramic tiles

plain, glazed ceramic tiles: shades of
green and beige

soft brush

cement-based tile adhesive

plastic spray bottle

cloths

1 On the back of the plywood, mark a point halfway across the width and a third from the top. Drill a rebate to fit under the keyhole of the mirror plate. Screw the plate in place and prime all sides of the board with diluted PVA (white) glue. Leave to dry, then score the front with a sharp implement such as a bradawl.

2 Measure the border tiles and draw a frame to match this size on the front of the board. Draw a simple tree or trace the template from the back of the book on to the centre. Cover the border of the board with PVA glue and stick the border tiles in position, placing them closely together.

3 Use tile nippers to cut the blue and white tiles into small, irregular shapes. Glue into place for the sky. Cut beige tiles for the trunk, glue face down on the board and prime with diluted glue. Cut and glue tiles for the leaves and earth. Leave to dry overnight.

4 Brush dry tile adhesive over the panel, filling all the gaps. Spray with water until saturated. When dry, repeat if necessary, then rub adhesive into the crevices, wiping off the excess. Dry overnight, then polish with a soft cloth.

This unusual and decorative dragonfly plaque is made from plywood and pieces of old china. Search market stalls and junk shops for old plates and saucers, and check your cupboards for rejects.

Dragonfly Plaque

You will need
tracing paper
pencil
5mm/¼in plywood, 50cm/20in square
jigsaw
bradawl
PVA (white) glue
paintbrush
acrylic primer
sandpaper
dark green acrylic paint
cable strippers
electric cable
wire cutters
selection of china
tile nippers
tile adhesive
coloured tile grout
brush
cloth

1 Enlarge the template provided and transfer it on to the plywood. Cut out the dragonfly and make two small hanging holes at the top of the body with a bradawl. Seal the front with diluted PVA (white) glue and the back with acrylic primer. When dry, sand the back and paint with green acrylic paint. Strip some electric cable and cut a short length of wire. Push this through the holes from the back and twist together securely.

2 Cut the china into regular shapes using tile nippers. Dip each piece into tile adhesive, scooping up a thick layer, and press down securely on the plywood to fill in the design. Leave to dry overnight.

3 Press grout into the gaps between the china. Leave it to dry for about 5 minutes, then brush off the excess. Leave for another 5 minutes, then polish with a cloth.

With a little work and imagination, this battered old chair has been transformed into an unusual, exciting piece of furniture. This example shows the extremes to which the medium can successfully be taken.

Crazy Paving Chair

You will need

wooden chair

2cm/¾in plywood (optional)

jigsaw (optional)

paint or varnish stripper

coarse-grade sandpaper

paintbrush

PVA (white) glue

wood glue

cement-based tile adhesive

admix

mixing container

flexible knife

pencil or chalk

large selection of china

tile nippers

dilute hydrochloric acid (optional)

soft cloth

1 If the chair you have chosen has a padded seat, remove it. There may be a wooden pallet beneath the padding which you can use as a base for the mosaic. If not, cut a piece of plywood to fit in its place.

2 Strip the chair of any paint or varnish and sand down with coarse-grade sandpaper. Then paint the whole chair with diluted PVA (white) glue to seal it.

4 Draw a design or motifs on any large flat surfaces of the chair with a pencil or chalk. Use simple shapes that are easy to read.

5 Select china that has colours and patterns to suit the motifs you have drawn. Using tile nippers, cut the china into the appropriate shapes and sizes.

3 When the surface is dry, stick the seat in place with a strong wood glue and fill any gaps around the edge with cement-based tile adhesive mixed with admix, which will provide extra strength and flexibility.

▶

6 Spread cement-based tile adhesive with admix within the areas of your design and press the cut china firmly into it.

7 Select china to cover the rest of the chair. As you are unlikely to have enough of the same pattern to cover the whole chair, choose two or three patterns that look good together.

8 Cut the china into small, varied shapes. Working on small areas at a time, tile the rest of the chair. Where one section of wood meets another, change the pattern of the china you are using.

9 Cut appropriately patterned china into thin slivers and use these to tile the edges of any thin sections of wood. Here, the edges of the back rest are covered. Leave for at least 24 hours to dry completely.

10 Mix up some more cement-based tile adhesive with the admix. Using a flexible knife, smooth this grout into the four corners of every piece of wood. Use your fingers to rub the grout over the flat surfaces. Work on a small area at a time and try to clean off most of the excess as you go. Leave overnight to dry.

11 Sand off the excess cement. This can be quite a difficult job, as there are many awkward angles. Alternatively, dilute hydrochloric acid can be used, but you must wear the appropriate protective clothing and apply it either outside or where there is good ventilation. Wash any residue from the surface with plenty of water and, when dry, polish with a soft cloth.

Templates

Enlarge the templates on a photocopier. Alternatively, trace the design and draw a grid of evenly spaced squares over your tracing. Draw a larger grid on to another piece of paper and copy the outline square by square. Finally, draw over the lines to make sure they are continuous.

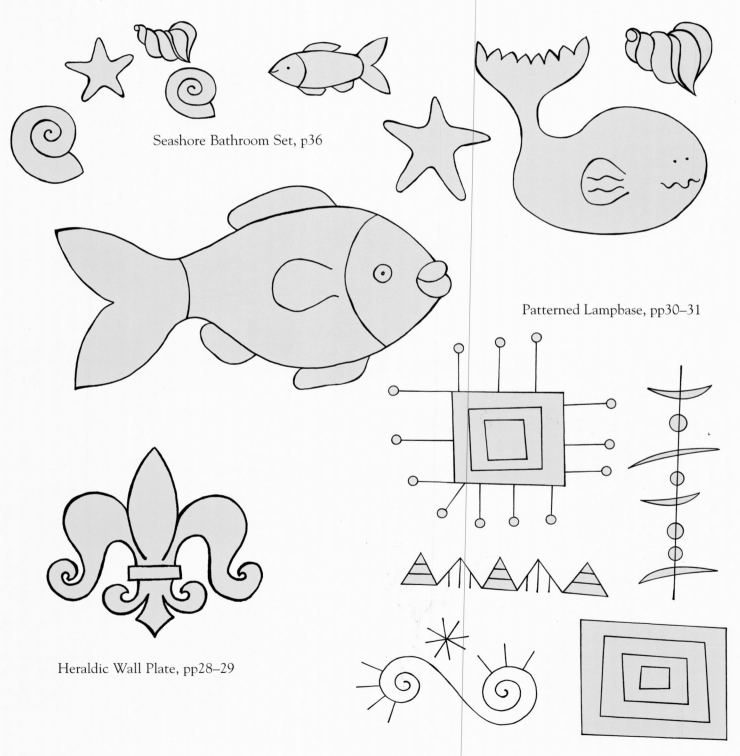

Seashore Bathroom Set, p36

Patterned Lampbase, pp30–31

Heraldic Wall Plate, pp28–29

Seashore-style China, pp20–21

Patterned Lampbase, pp30–31

Fun Bunnies Tea Set, pp42–43

Morning Sun Face, p37

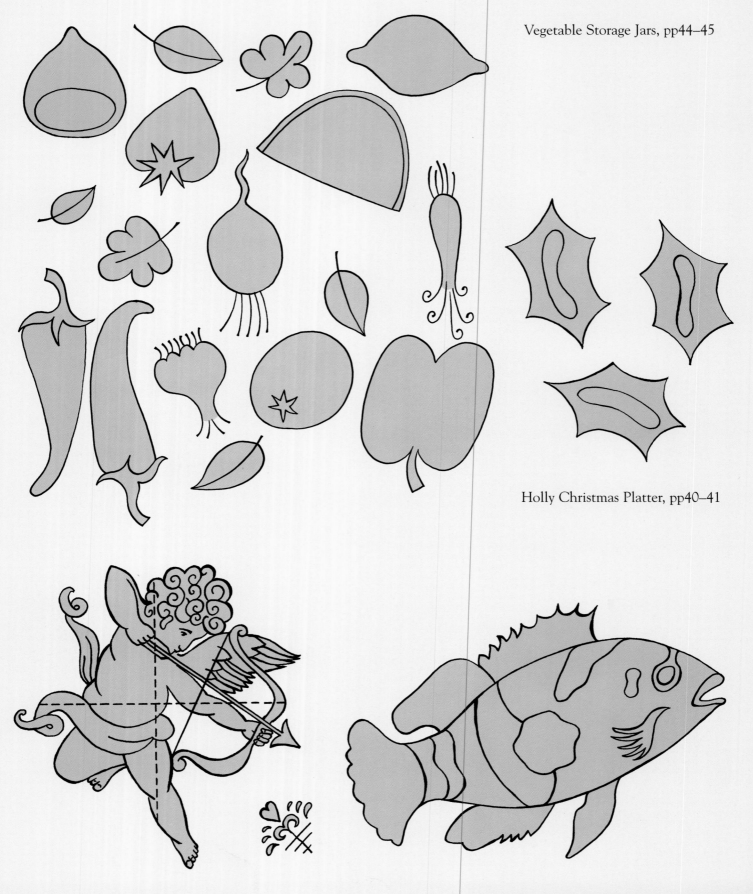

Vegetable Storage Jars, pp44–45

Holly Christmas Platter, pp40–41

Cherub Tiles, pp64–65

Maritime Tile Mural, pp62–63

Floral Tiles, p66

Italianate Tiles, p67

Majolica Tiles, p68

Cartoon Tiles, p59

Byzantine Bird Tile, p69

Art Nouveau Tiles, pp72–73

William Morris Tiles, pp78–79

Sgraffito
Fish Tiles, p60

Folk Art Cabinet, pp126–127

Alhambra Picture Frame, p104

Lemonade Pitcher, pp102–103

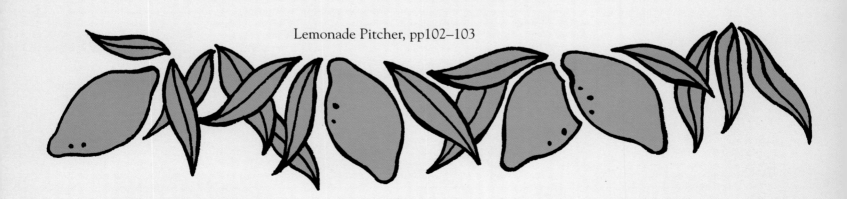

Venetian Perfume Bottle, pp124–125

Sunlight Catcher, pp100–101

Leaf Photograph Frame, pp96–97

Folk Art Glass, pp122–123

Bohemian Bottle, pp120–121

French-lavender Flower Vase, pp118–119

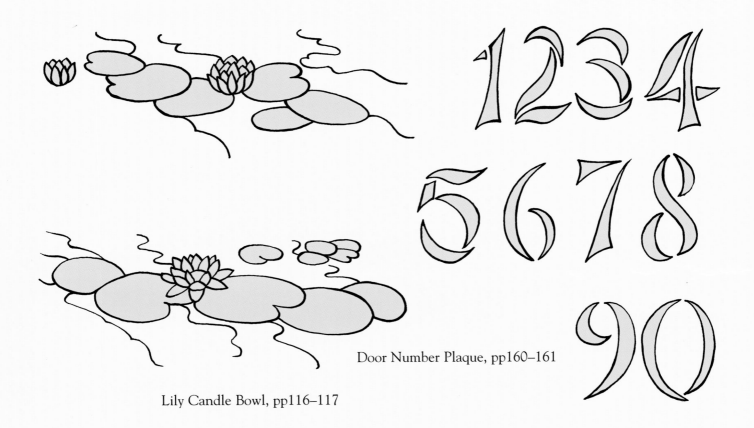

Door Number Plaque, pp160–161

Lily Candle Bowl, pp116–117

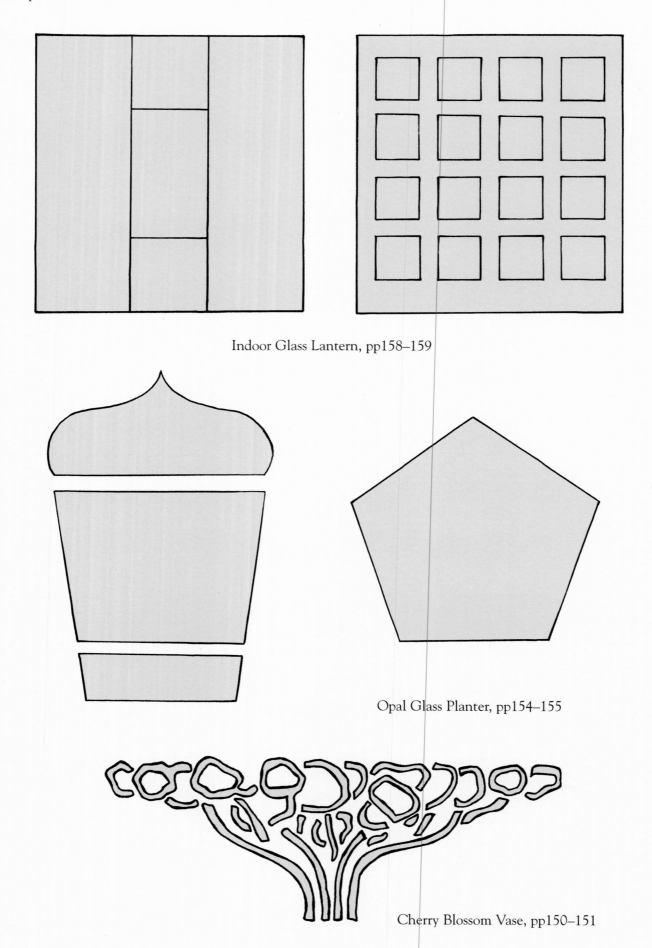

Indoor Glass Lantern, pp158–159

Opal Glass Planter, pp154–155

Cherry Blossom Vase, pp150–151

Window Hanging, pp162–163

Trinket Box, pp166–168

Heart Light Catcher, pp144–145

Curtain Decorations, pp164–165

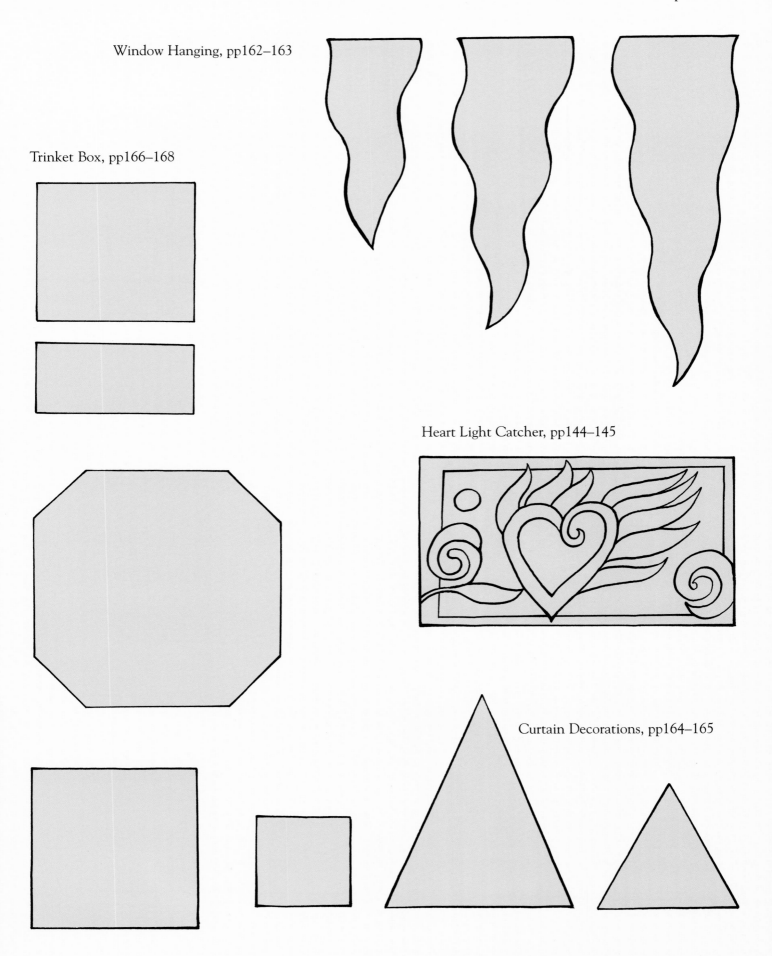

Bathroom Cabinet Door Panel, pp169–171

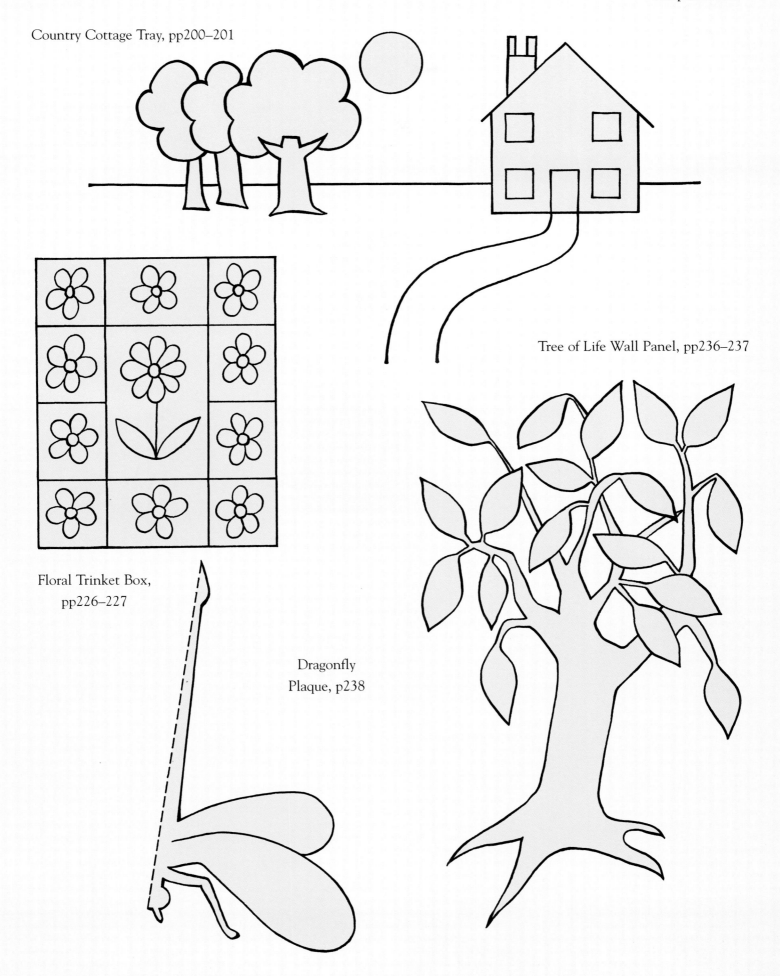

Country Cottage Tray, pp200–201

Floral Trinket Box,
pp226–227

Tree of Life Wall Panel, pp236–237

Dragonfly
Plaque, p238

254

Index

Acknowledgements

The publisher would like to thank the following people for designing projects in this book:

Helen Baird for the Jazzy Plant Pot, Mosaic Bottle, Country Cottage Tray, Mosaic Table, Garden Urn, Tree of Life Wall Panel, Spiral Lamp Stand, Floral Trinket Box, Spiral Vase, Boat Splashback, Mosaic Bedhead and Crazy Paving Chair.

Michael Ball for the Lemonade Jug, Alhambra Picture Frame, Folk Art Cabinet, Lily Candle Bowl, Banded Vase, Door Number Plaque, Opal Glass Planter, Cherry Blossom Vase and Window Hanging.

Emma Biggs for the Abstract Mirror

Petra Boase for the Mexican Folk Art Tiles and Frosted Vase.

Tessa Brown for the Love Letter Rack.

Anna-Lise De'Ath for the Sun Light Catcher, Patterned Bathroom Bottle, Leaded Picture Frames, Leaded Door Panels and Mosaic Lantern.

Marion Elliot for the Roman Numeral Tiles, Byzantine Bird Tile, Pueblan Tiles, Underwater Panel and Silver Decoupage Tiles.

Mary Fellows for the Alphabet Tiles, Cartoon Tiles, Autumn Leaf Coffee Pot, Heart Decoration, Geometric Bordered Frame and Stained Glass Window.

Lucinda Ganderton for the Morning Sun Face, Art Nouveau Tiles, Floral Tiles, Italianate Tiles, Majolica Tile, William Morris Tiles, Venetian Perfume Bottle, Leaf Photograph Frame, Bohemian Bottle, and

French-lavender Flower Vase.

Sandra Hadfield for the Door Number Plaque and Mosaic Fire Screen.

Lesley Harle for the Heraldic Wall Plate, Low-relief Jug and Holly Christmas Platter.

Susie Johns for the Christmas Baubles.

Francesca Kaye for the Rosebud Tiles.

Izzy Moreau for the Stamped Spongeware and Maritime Tile Mural.

Helen Musselwhite for the Seashore Bathroom Set, Patterned Lamp Base, Fun Bunnies Tea Set and Vegetable Storage Jars.

Cleo Mussi for the Plant Pots, Sunflower Mosaic, Arched Mirror, Decorative Spheres, China Tiles, Mosaic Garden Table and Dragonfly Plaque.

Deidre O'Malley for the Glass Nugget Window Hanging, Indoor Glass Lantern and Curtain Decorations.

Emma Micklethwaite for the

Bathroom Cabinet Door Panel.

Joanna Nevin for the Stained Glass Screen.

Cheryl Owen for the Champagne Flutes and Butterfly Bowl.

Marie Perkins for the Sgraffito Fish Tiles, Citrus Fruit Bowl, Kitchen Herb Jars and Sunflower Vase.

Polly Plouviez for the Kitchen Storage Jar, Painted Salt and Pepper Pots and Glass Nugget Bottle Holder

Debbie Siniska for the Heart Light Catcher.

Tanya Siniska for the Flowers and Foliage Wallhanging.

Andrea Spencer for the Seashore-style China.

Isabel Stanley for the Leaf Motif Cup and Saucer, Fish Splashback.

Norma Vondee for the Aztec Box.

Stewart Walton for the Folk Art Glass.